I0429715

How to Turn Mundane
Into Magnificent!

Easy, Affordable DIY Ideas to Transform Your Home

By Alexa Keating

Prologue

We have all heard the axiom that the longest journey begins with the first step; I believe it is begins before that.

I believe that when something matters to us a lot, we harbor a dream, so dare to dream. The dream fans a tiny flame, a pilot light that ignites hope. Hope springs to life when we begin to believe that there might be a way to accomplish the dream. Once we believe in the dream, we begin to realize that dream.

"You can start with nothing. And out of nothing, and out of no way, a way will be made"

- Michael Beckwith

Introduction

'How to Turn Mundane into Magnificent' is the third release in the 'Make It Mine' series.

This book goes transcends home decorating as it delves into the nuts and bolts of how to make all those projects happen!

'How to Turn Mundane into Magnificent' is step-by-step guide that helps you discover the look and feel you want to create in your home.

The common sense theory from the 'Make It Mine' book continues here as we examine how to use what you have, to do what you can, where you are; creating an entirely new look on a minimal budget. It provides a wonderful, lighthearted approach to repurposing your furnishings and accessories and redecorating your home or apartment!

Every home is a personal expression of the people who live there. 'How to Turn Mundane into Magnificent' guides you ever so subtly, as you delve into your family's lifestyle, helping you to decide exactly what you need from the space and what you really want to create in your home. Once you have determined your goal, this book will lead you effortlessly (almost!) to your objective.

The book is filled with information on how to identify the features of each room, and then defines the best and most cost effective way to make the room work with your new plan. Next we help you select the best pieces of your existing furniture and how to find the best prices for second hand selections that will act to create your new decorating ideas in a stunning finished project.

Refinishing furniture and repurposing accessories becomes easy and fun as you transform old, tired items into the perfect new look in your space; for pennies!

'How to Turn Mundane into Magnificent' shares hundreds of ideas to help you improve your home; in today's economy this is a must read! 'How to Turn Mundane into Magnificent' is the new 'survival bible' for recreating spaces in your home.

It is filled with money saving ideas, space planning, profound thoughts, inspiration and practical ideas for successful living.

Table of Contents

Prologue

Introduction

Dedication

Chapter 1   Now What?   8

Chapter 2   That Scoundrel 'Not Me!'   15

Chapter 3   When Chaos is King!   18

Chapter 4   Know Thyself!   34

Chapter 5   Color Your World   45

Chapter 6   Looking Into You   63

Chapter 7   Into Your Light   85

Chapter 8   Ushering In Your Luck   101

Chapter 9   A Change Is Gonna Come!   111

Chapter 10 Sizing It Up!   229

Chapter 11 Barely Get Along Street Rocks   245

Chapter 12 A Diva Divers Treasure Hunt   252

Chapter 13 The Heart of Your Home   274

Chapter 14 About That Bath!   300

Chapter 15 The First Step In the Journey   317

Chapter 16 Living With Your Choices   321

Chapter 17 Into Your Night   332

Chapter 18 Guess The Guest   339

Chapter 19 Kids Are People Too!   347

Chapter 20   It's a Family Affair   352

Chapter 21 Wide Open Places   354

Chapter 22   Crowded Spaces Lonely Places   367

Chapter 23 Access Accessories   374

Chapter 24 Tools for our Trade   392

Chapter 25 Know When To Fold 'Em   394

Chapter 26 The Hero in You   402

            How to Paint Your Rooms

            How to Paint Your Floors

            Wallpapering FAQ'S

            Furniture Placement Guidelines

            About the Author

Dedication

This book was inspired by and written for all the people who wish they could create their dream home, have limited funds to commit to your ideas, and don't quite know where to start or how to make it happen!

This is not just an instructional manual; it is more like a best friend who works side by side with you to bring your dreams to culmination. There's a difference.

You have inspired me and many others to reach higher, and grow farther in the search to help create new ideas and better methods; once unheard of.

To all of our 'Make it Mine' warriors who jumped in, and dared to dream and to act, your shared thoughts and questions prompted me to take another step forward in helping you to complete those plans and projects. I'm proud of you! You will be too!

Chapter 1
Now What?

This seems to be the number one question for everyone who takes a long look around their living space and wonders how it all came to this!

We begin with such vast hopes and dreams, go shopping in various places or collect hand me downs from a relative only to end up with a result that screams 'not me!' Or worse, you look around at a room full of odds and ends and what, in your eyes, appears to be 'early junk' furniture and decide you hate it all; a second look at your expendable income that can be used to transform the room into something that feels desirable leaves you feeling rather hopeless.

Take heart! This is where the fun begins. This book is designed to help you take a thoughtful approach to each room in your home. Together we will decide exactly what the purpose of the room is going to be, what you need the room to accomplish in your home, what 'look and feel' suits you and your lifestyle best. Next we will take a new look at what you have to work with to create the ideal space. Then, we go to work!

Some thoughts to remember before we begin; visiting a home for the first time and meeting the people who live there, I discovered a few things that seem to be the 'norm' in every home.

Some pieces of furniture and accessories are sacred. They were given to you by someone special and you plan to never let them go, no matter what. You may be open to re purposing them into something magnificent when we are finished.

There are a few pieces of furniture and accessories that you picked up at yard sales, thrift stores or bought from a friend as you began your decorating plan. We can do great things with these!

There are some new pieces of furniture and accessories that you fell in love with or got a great deal on but they just don't look the way you hoped they would. We will determine where these pieces can shine in your plan.

You had a lot of this 'stuff' before you moved into this space. This book will help you make a decision about what can be used, what can be re purposed and what you may want to sell to acquire the funds for new pieces you consider a 'must have.'

If any of these statements apply to you and your home, consider yourself 'normal.' A cautionary note; there is an issue that is perhaps not so much the 'norm' but makes life very uncomfortable in our homes; a husband with one very distinct style that makes him feel comfortable and a wife with a completely different style. Typically, each of these partners believes their style is best. This kind of situation can create so much conflict in your home that no style ever develops; many times it actually escalates to a place where one of the partners has begun to question their own sense of style or has given up on gaining control of their surroundings to avoid arguments or painful interaction. This can feel defeating.

If this is your situation I urge you to select a room that both of you have agreed is under your control; a space that is either not shared (like a bedroom) or a space where you spend the primary amount of time and therefore can be expected to gain some control over the character of the room.

Later we will address the other members in your household and how to include them in the plans. This day, we are rediscovering YOU!

Choose A Room; Any Room!

If you are unsure where to start, begin where you are the most uncomfortable in your home; a space that makes you feel unwelcome, is uninviting and even perhaps just plain ugly. That's the one!

You may even find yourself in a situation where you have no choice; things have to change! This typically comes about when you have a new addition to your household or something has changed like children in college who need a different kind of space, a new job that requires an office to work from, elderly parents moving in or all of your children leaving the nest. Suddenly you need something different to make the home more user friendly. There are all kinds of reasons but if this is your situation then you already know where to start.

Your mission will be far easier if you are able to clear the room of all of the furniture and accessories. If that is not possible, move everything to the center of the room and visually 'clear the room.'

Grab a tablet to make notes and your favorite drink and find a comfortable place to sit down. You may like sitting on the floor in a sunbeam!

This is the beginning of a journey that will take you step-by-step from A to Z and will result in a finished room that is totally YOU!

Take a deep breath and look around you. Notice the natural lighting that is available in the room, which direction the windows are facing, where the doorways are and any 'unusual' features in your room. Make a note of these issues. Unusual here is defined as any wall that is broken by closets, built-ins or anything else that prevents the wall from being a straight wall. This is important!

Some examples of challenging architectural designs are:

Irregular shapes with fireplace oddly jutting out
Irregular shaped rooms
Angular and unusable spaces
Odd, narrow corners and excessive doors in a bedroom
Triangle shapes from bedroom entry
Fireplace stuck in the corner by a door
Angled ceilings, tiny spaces

Bay windows in an inconvenient location
Narrow unusable room converted to bath

Long, narrow open spaces (typically found in Cape Cod Style home or a home where the attic was finished out. These typically have a dormer area transformed into an attractive and functional space.

Now decide whether you want those nooks and crannies to be hidden or whether you want to emphasize them. If they are attractive or give the room character, I like to show them off. If they reflect a completely different style than the one you choose for the room, you may want to intentionally ignore them. You decide how they make you feel and that will be the right premise for you to work from.

If you find that your personal style is contemporary or minimalist you will most likely feel more comfortable allowing these unusual spaces to blend into the décor rather than showcasing them. Paint color, floor treatments, window treatments and furniture placement all work together to create the style you choose.

Even though it may be difficult, at this point you may be better off to ignore the furniture. If you focus on the furniture you might find yourself determining your personal style by what you see in the room and what you believe you have to work with.

It is an easy trap to fall into; don't do it! This is a new awakening. Treat it like the first day of your life. We are going to begin again and this time, we will create your dream. Be at peace, be calm; we are going to rediscover YOU now!

Chapter 2
That Scoundrel, 'Not Me!'

I have had the opportunity to meet many people on my life path. Every single person has had an encounter with 'not me.'

You meet this scoundrel at work when something is missing and no one moved it, at home when you suddenly find mud caked on the white carpet and in a multitude of other places along the way. Wherever something has happened and no one want to assume responsibility for the actions, you'll find he's been there; the one and only 'not me.' We can live with that out there in the world, but who let him into our home?

If things feel unbalanced or out of control in our lives, it is frequently reflected in our homes. Likewise, if we want to correct that in our lives, the home is the best place to begin. Why? Because it is our refuge; your home is the place where you lock out the intruders in your life and let your hair down. It is a sacred sanctity where we go for inner healing and peace of mind. These things are essential to our happiness. When balance is absent in our life we begin to feel despair and soon the best parts of ourselves, including the creativity and joy we used to know, are lost. This is more true now than ever, as we are faced with dwindling jobs, rising gas prices, skyrocketing grocery costs, utility costs that climb monthly and a multitude of other challenges that may not be our fault. We have all begun to feel a little bit victimized by these daily challenges. These are created by the ultimate 'Not Me.' Even if you can identify the cause, you don't have a lot of control over the cure.

Many people lose their jobs, find they are suddenly single unexpectedly or are forced to endure a completely unexpected life altering change.

If you find yourself in a new place that feels like anything but home, or if you have spent the last few years trying to survive and have been afraid to spend anything to create a better space to live, know that you are not alone.

This is happening to millions of people. We feel overwhelmed and suddenly we begin to examine how this happened to our lives and our homes. We miss the childhood dreams that have vanished with the years and our self-esteem that has been corrupted by a universal failure not of our making. Suddenly, it seems like our potential has been bartered for security.

We're starting over… right here, in this room with the very things we have to work with, we are going to begin again.

What do all these very big issues have to do with your home? Everything! Your home is a reflection of how you see yourself! It is the one point of beginning where you do have control and you can determine the outcome.

"We cannot have anything materialize in life that we are not willing to become in consciousness."

~ Michael Beckwith

Thoughts are powerful; words are action!

'Not Me!' is the alter ego of 'Chaos Is King.' It is essential to identify issues before we can solve them.

Chapter 3
When Chaos is King

This book is an opportunity to get to know ourselves, again. To take stock of where we really are and how we are going to get to the place we want to go. So, take heed! Look around; if the things in this chapter do not seem to apply to you and your home, I bet you know someone this glove fits!

Chaos in a home is evident when there is no specific place for shoes, clothing, books, TV remotes and a host of other things.

I can't tell you how many times I have walked into a home like this and listened to the host who relates one of the following causes:

a) "No one listens; the kids refuse to help and I can't do this by myself."

b) "My partner won't help! He or she is a slob and has no respect for the things that are important to me."

c) "I'm busy! I don't have time to be a slave to a house."

d) "I'm no maid; why should I pick up after everyone? No one does it for me!"

e) "I don't care. Houses are just not that important to me!"

f) "I had to clean house all of my life! My mother made me clean hers and my kids can do ours!" (More common that you know) Imagine hearing, "This house is a mess! The kids haven't cleaned yet!" And, it feels right to the person who is saying this to you.

g) "I spent a lot of years getting my education and degree; I have way too much on the ball to worry about housework". (This is a VIP syndrome)

h) "I hate housework! Who cares?"

There are lot's more; these are the ones I most frequently hear. Catch a clue here; these people have some things in common!

1) There is an underlying anger issue in nearly every statement. Someone feels used or abused!

2) People are confused about time issues; what takes their time and what wastes their time.

3) Declining health issues have begun and normal maintenance, upkeep and housekeeping have become too difficult to perform.

4) Most people who have chaos in their home are overwhelmed. They can't 'see the reaching' and the task seems daunting. What's the use of digging in if it won't make a difference?

5) There is usually chaos in some other important area of the lives of people who choose to live like this. Your surroundings reflect your state of consciousness.

Your home is the biggest investment you will likely make and the one place charged with providing comfort to you and your family.

That's why it is referred to as your castle in general; and why the US Constitution takes so much care to protect your rights with respect to your home.

It's important! Let's find the method to make you fall in love with it again!

One by one, let's examine the most typical 'reasons' people provide; then we can visit getting a new perspective on this issue!

Solutions to Consider

a)"No one listens; the kids refuse to help and I can't do this by myself."

Chaos, in and of itself, creates the 'no one listens' attitude. Everyone feels overwhelmed, no one knows where to start and no one can see the finish line.

Therefore, everyone refuses to waste their time helping achieve something they believe is not possible. This becomes a habit! After some time passes it becomes, "This is how we live."

Whose Job Is It?

'This is a story about 4 people named Everybody, Somebody, Anybody and Nobody. There was an important job to be done and everybody was sure somebody would do it. Anybody could have done it, but nobody did it. Somebody got angry about that, because it was

Everybody's job. Everybody thought anybody could do it but Nobody realized that Everybody wouldn't do it. It ended up that everybody blamed Somebody when Nobody did what Anybody could have done.'

~ Author Unknown

Someone has to 'step up' and begin the change process. It is a little tougher when you are feeling overwhelmed but things happen quickly once you commit to it.

One at a time – this is the process. I like to start at the front door; you choose your most important starting point.

Many people who exhibit the 'It's no one's business how my house looks' attitude scoff at the front door process. I can't understand why these people don't see that they and their family use the same door! Who doesn't want to be warmly welcomed at their front door?

If you can't imagine where to start I like to empty the room. Leave the furniture if you don't have the space to move it out, but move it to the center of the room. Then clear the room, pictures and all.

It's a new point of beginning. Look at the walls and windows. This is a great time to take stock of wall colors.

Preview the next chapter 'Color Your World' for an in depth look at colors and how they affect everyone in the room including the first impression. Soothing neutral earth tone colors set the tone of warmth and coziness. If you don't have one on your walls try to find $20.00 in your budget and buy paint.

Clean the woodwork and windowsills, and then move to the windows. Sparkling clean windows allows natural light to penetrate the gloom.

Clean the floor. Then tackle the overhead lighting or fans. The 'Light IN Your Life' chapter is devoted to how to select lighting that fits your personal style and budget and creates the feeling you want to inspire in your room.

A lack of storage is the chief offender in chaos. Either you can't find it or never used it! It's time.

First take a long and honest look at the things you have removed from your room. What falls into the 'clutter' pile and what is important to you?

Eliminate the clutter. I find it to be easier to leave it in the pile I have moved out of the room and follow this process until every room is finished. Then make the final decision as to whether it is a 'must keep item' or can leave your life gracefully.

Check out the Furniture Placement chapter in this book and get some ideas as to how it affects the room.

Look at what you want to create and then be bold! Try some different furniture placement ideas and find the one that best suits you.

After the first room is complete, this becomes a natural process to move through the home and eliminate chaos and clutter. So dig in!

b) "My partner won't help! He or she is a slob and has no respect for the things that are important to me."

This is one of those underlying anger issues we talked about!

It is work examining why you feel that way and why your partner chooses to ignore your feelings.

Come to an agreement that is respectful to both of you and make a commitment to honor the agreement.

Then visit the a) No One Listens solutions above and dig in to alter the course of chaos and regain your peace of mind.

c) "I'm busy! I don't have time to be a slave to a house."

Imagine that! You have time to spend needless wasted hours hunting for important papers, shoes, lost clothing, keys and a multitude of other important things you need.

This causes countless explanations to others beginning with the 'I can't find it but as soon as I locate it I'll let you know' story to the 'It's gone; I don't know how that is possible but I've looked everywhere to no avail' excuse.

You're too busy? Seriously; you're too busy?

Visit the 'a) No One Listens' solutions section and recover hours of wasted time. If you're really busy you don't have time to waste on needless searches. You've become a slave to your unwillingness to participate in your own success.

Getting order back into your home will bring order to your life. Things just get simple and you'll have a lot more time to spend on the things you want to squeeze into your schedule.

d) "I'm no maid; why should I pick up after everyone? No one does it for me!"

This is another underlying anger issue! No one wants to feel like a maid in their own home. No one wants to be the only one who cares about things being in place either.

There is a sense of unfairness playing out here. If this is how you really feel it is time for a family council meeting. Every member of the household should attend; let everyone 'vent' their own feelings.

Every person in the home is entitled to some measure of respect for their feelings, even the children. If you instill the attitude that respect is important at a young age your children will never forget it as they grow into adulthood. It is a valuable characteristic.

Then begin to form an agreement about how the family would like their space to feel and how to arrive at that point.

No matter what the reasons are, unless you are addressing a specific room and the occupant's unwillingness to perform duties, everyone will probably begin at the point of 'a) No One Listens.'

Visit that section and follow the ideas there when you are ready to begin.

e) "I don't care. How my home looks is just not that important to me!"

I wonder why? You are willing to spend a large part of your income to supply a roof over your head and yet, it's just not that important.

Examine why you feel that way. Everyone dreams of having their own space, a private place to call 'mine.' If you feel your home is not important, you may want to reconsider this one. Many times it really means, 'I am overwhelmed and do not know where to start!' Studies in human nature have proven that if we don't know what to do this will usually result in doing nothing.

Take heart; revisit the a)' No One Listens' solutions above and start reclaiming control of your space. You'll be glad you did!

f) "I had to clean house all of my life! My mother made me clean hers and my kids can clean mine!" (This is more common than you know) Imagine hearing, "This house is a mess! The kids haven't cleaned it yet!" And, it feels right to the person who is saying this to you.

This one is particularly disturbing to me. Imagine how many times a day we say, "You're just a child, you can't make those kinds of decisions."

And yet, the most important investment of our lives is turned over to the same children who are too young to decide what to have on their dinner plate.

If your parents placed you in this position, remember how overwhelmed it made you feel.

Many times families encounter abrupt changes; divorce, death of a parent or illness of one of the parents, and things change quickly. It may seem natural to just 'let the kids' do the tasks.

For a temporary solution this may be fine; tell them it is temporary and why it is. And then, look for help from family or friends for the things you cannot do.

I hope you will reconsider this position and step up and reclaim the adult part of this responsibility.

If not, you may create generations of emotionally abused children who grow up resentful and angry about their homes instead of appreciating the opportunity to claim personal space and enjoy it.

I urge you to visit the 'a) No One listens' solutions and bring the family together by providing a well loved place to call home.

g) "I spent a lot of years getting my education and degree; I have way too much on the ball to worry about housework." (This is a VIP syndrome)

You may be surprised at how many people parrot this attitude.

If keeping this attitude is important to you, then I sincerely hope you have managed to turn all that education into enough income to pay someone else to maintain control of your home.

That is, if you are willing to turn the reins over to someone else. I'm not. Rarely do people have 'too much on the ball' to live in harmony in their home.

Examine this attitude closely; maybe you just need to think about what is really important to you and then prioritize your home at or near the top of the list.

You also need to visit 'a) No One Listens' for solutions and either dig in yourself or supervise someone else in the process.

You have way too much on the ball to live in chaos and disorder that wastes your time. This thought process will work wonders for you.

She was very important!

I once showed up for an open house at a home where the woman of the home felt this way.

Dirty socks and clothing were strewn throughout the home, dishes were piled up so high it was impossible to see the counter space, there was an unpleasant odor throughout the home – one that smelled of grime; bathrooms were revolting and bedrooms were piled high with clutter. Only the bed was open and readily accessible, although unmade.

While it certainly was not my job to clean house I was embarrassed to even allow potential buyers in the door. A call to my Sales Manager made it clear that I had to stay because the Open House ad was in the paper. For obvious reasons, the home had been on the market for a very long time with no interest. The owner apparently had no interest either!

I spent several minutes picking up the clutter from the floors, ran the dishwater and piled the dirty dishes into the sink, vacuumed the floors, mopped the tiled areas and proceeded to clean bathrooms and wash dishes.

I decided I had pretty much taken over the home at that point so I strategically positioned the furniture.

I was scheduled for a three hour open house; five lookers came through while I was in the process of cleaning it up, and one buyer who saw the finished project. I worked hard for that commission!

The owner should have done the same things months ago and they would have been happily ensconced in their new home much sooner!

There is a little bit of arrogance in this attitude that I always question when I encounter it.

I also have a good education, and I'm sharp enough to know that this kind of clutter and dirt doesn't 'feel' good!

h) "I hate housework! Who cares?"

I've learned that once chaos and disorder are eliminated in a home; all the occupants regain respect for the way it looks and feels.

Why? Because they have regained the lost time searching for things that are never in place because they had no place; and, have honestly enjoyed how their home feels to them and to everyone who comes through the door. It instills a sense of pride. And that's a good thing!

Let's take a moment to look at other causes:

Declining health issues may have begun and normal maintenance, upkeep and housekeeping have become too difficult to perform.

Elderly people do not like to let others know how hard things have become for them.

It makes them feel even more helpless which is very frightening; they already have begun to see their independence and control of their lives slipping away.

Pay close attention if you notice things are not the same in an elderly persons home. They may be quietly screaming for help and afraid to speak out.

If so, round up the most caring people in their lives and make a plan, with them, to help do the things that you know are important to them on a regular basis.

People who become unexpectedly handicapped feel the same way.

This happens with aging or accidents or a multitude of unexpected events. Handicapped people usually wonder why no one else has noticed what they can't do, but they are too proud, or in too much pain to speak up.

Chapter 4
Know Thyself

The best place to begin to find out what really appeals to you is by defining your decorating style This is the key to creating a room that really reflects the essence of you. If this sounds impossible, fear not! You can readily identify the look you crave.

1.) Look at your furniture. With a pad in hand, walk from room to room and make two truthful lists: "Love It" and "Wish I Could Replace It." Catalog everything you can, including art—just be honest. It's all based on how things make you feel.

2.) Gather the items you cherish. Check the top of your dresser, your mantel, and your bookshelves; then pull special clothes from your closet. Take a long look at the items, and make note of those that make you feel beautiful and joyful.

3.) Think about places you love and why you love them. "Picture your dream home, if you could live anywhere. How would it look? Does it have high ceilings, arches, lots of windows? Is it cozy and comfortable or sophisticated and beautiful? Then think outside of home: "If you were invited to the Oscars, what would you wear?" This moves you beyond the limitations of your lifestyle and budget and into a new realm of creativity.

4.) Look for common threads—design, colors, shapes, materials, vibe—among the things you treasure. See which of the styles pictured here that your picks most jibe with. You may find yourself attracted to a blend of styles rather than just one; as you delve into the following rooms, note which features appeal to you. This will help you translate your taste into smart decorating choices. Now let's see what your list reflects.

Sophisticated Classic

This style is an elegant blend of refined traditional furniture, jewelry-like accessories, and pale hues. Patrician old-world elements pair with cleaner Art Deco shapes. The look evokes a more formal lifestyle. When defining Sophisticated Classic, think Grace Kelly, Tiffany & Co., and

Charlotte from Sex and the City when defining this style.

Modern Graphic

Modern Graphic is a fresh, fun, contemporary look that combines urban styling (imagine a downtown loft) with edgy, colorful elements and midcentury design. Simple furniture forms balance out bold accents and patterns. Think the Museum of Modern Art, Frank Lloyd Wright, and a Rubik's Cube.

Cozy Casual

A warm, traditional look made for relaxing with family and friends. This style draws on English and early-American furniture designs, as well as laid-back country, cottage, and farmhouse styles. Weathered, low-maintenance furnishings are easy, inviting, and built for daily life. Think golden retrievers, fuzzy slippers, and just about any movie that reflects a Rockwell Painting theme.

Vintage Eclectic

A rich, layered look combining flea-market finds, furniture designs from various time periods (including Victorian pieces and 18th-century French styles), and a diverse collection of accessories and artwork. Dusty colors, timeworn or handmade textiles, and collected objects create a lived-in feel. Think Paris flea markets, Granny's teacups, the film Grey Gardens.

Victorian Styles

Luxurious, ornate and comfortable, the Victorian interior spaces bathe in nobility and class, showing off expensive fabrics and elaborate pieces of furniture. Here is what designers like to call the most luxurious, gilded design style which surprisingly is, at the same time, cozy and comfortable.

Victorian Architecture - Architectural components such as coving arches, cornicing and ceilings are considered key elements in obtaining the Victorian aspect. You can easily turn your plain room surfaces into Victorian masterpieces with specific decorative details like bas-reliefs with nature motifs, carvings and moldings.

Modern Minimalist Style

This style is a form of extreme accuracy; nothing is too much, without heavy backgrounds. The emphasis is on simplicity, the colors may be dull or bright, in any case flashy colors. Pieces are either geometric shapes – square, rectangular, round, but the surfaces are clean, no scenery, no details. Minimalist modern style by its name, illustrates the simplified forms.

Rustic Style

This style structure features crude, rough details, with structural elements of furniture. Lighting can be created from tree trunks, logs, branches, jute. This design is typically found in mountain vacation homes and rural areas.

Classic Reinterpreted Style

This is a refined style, elegant style, where classic forms details are found in a new approach. The forms preserves the structure of old forms or parts in general, updating them sometimes; or some elements of a furniture style may be combined with modern elements, creating that fusion between old and new. Finishing parts are in a new approach-painted and varnished, with different and innovative colors, surface gold, silver, finished with patina or serigraphic.

Maverick Style

The Maverick Style is a part of modern style; this approach is very inventive, unusual and unconventional. It reflects a personality that is young, explosive, and inventive and does not respect the rules. The structure can be obtained by joining pieces, or overlapping volumes and volumes. Twisting colors can be randomly chosen even for the same room, seemingly nothing happens. This is just a part of the eccentricity reflected in this style.

Contemporary Style

The style is really a contemporary-modern style but maintains a hot look through selected finishes and color ranges used. The finished look is a very new, modern, and cool design. Colors are balanced; warm, bright tones and pastels are out of the question when it comes to this style. Finishes are warm, wood-veneer, solid wood doors with frames or appearance to look more polished and panels upholstered with leather sometimes. These fabrics are characteristic of this style.

High-tech Style

High-tech style is an innovative modern style, the emphasis being on furniture structure where every detail of combination is not random and it is part of that structure.

Screws, rivets, wheels apparent booms, rough metal finishes, appearances bulbs are specific to this style. The finishes used are often of metal, glass and plastic and wood in small proportions and for parts we find fabric-upholstered as simple as we can, leather. The colors are often dull-gray, white, small black scale.

Elegant Country Style

Rural style is elegant furniture style with influences from English, French or Scandinavian classic pure style can be called rural chic. Furniture finishes are nice, bright colors-white, pastel colors and forms were taking over traditional furniture but not abundant decorations. Surfaces are painted or sometimes have a slight patina.

Shabby Chic

Soft floral fabrics and accessories, pale colors, and a mix of old and new define Shabby Chic Style decor. Shabby Chic Style Furniture features time-worn, romantic styling and solid construction, making them just right for those in search of this casual, comfortable style!

Shabby Seaside

A little more sophisticated in design; the seaside shabby incorporates more substantial metals reflected in the lantern lighting, accessories and chandeliers. Think casual, polished and sleek with lightweight window treatments that billow in the breeze.

Southwestern

Southwestern interior design is characterized rich texture, earth-tone colors as the main palette (with bright accents of yellow, orange, red clay, and turquoise), hand-crafted objects, and terra cotta or clay tile roofs. Upholstery is predominantly made of woven fabrics, leather and suede's as well as animal hides. Traditional native clothing and blankets may be used as wall décor.

Wood furniture is popular and may also feature a distressed finish with metal accents. Accents can be anything from hand-painted tiles to painted ceramic pieces with roots in 16th century Mexico.

Colonial (Mid Century)

This is the style used by the first settlers to America going back to the 17th Century.

It is also very similar to the 'New England' style of decorating. The first settlers came from England, so naturally they were very influenced by the styles of design and architecture which were around in England itself at that time. The lifestyle of the first settlers was very different from the established lifestyles and towns of England.

The first settlers had to build and create everything themselves, by hand so the style they used was simple and straight-forward and they made use of local building materials and techniques – which they used to create English-style designs.

Colonial decorating was rustic, basic and simple. But the period this decorating style covers lasted for around 300 years – so as time went on, and for richer people, the style became more ornate and lavish.

Island Colonial

In today's world we have learned to refer to this style as 'Tommy Bahama' or Caribbean style. Alas, it sprung from the British Colonies and morphed into Island Colonial!

Especially in the colonies of the British West Indies, color palettes for walls and window treatments typically reflected the lush colors found in nature: the vivid blues of the ocean and sky; the deeper greens of tree foliage and the rich pastels of flowering plants; and the varied yellows of sand

and sun. Botanical prints are common fabrics for bed benches, curtains, bedding sets and upholstered occasional chairs.

Beach Colonial

Goodness how times change! Even ten years ago we would have seen this style in a traditional home and recognized it. Not so today!

Notice the changes in today's look. White walls, white bead board on the walls and at the ceiling; it is used as trim in place of the old school crown molding! The use of very light weight fabrics hint at the ocean breeze; the use of shuttered window and door treatments permits the doors to remain open to the ocean breeze and yet keep the mosquitoes out!

Contemporary Colonial

This seems like a contradiction but here it is! The high arched windows combined with the old pomp and circumstance found in traditional Victorian styles have now transformed into a contemporary colonial. This is reminiscent for the Italian Renaissance era!

Regardless, notice the mixture of modern sofas, traditional chairs, Victorian desks and Chrystal chandeliers to add elegance and beauty.

Chapter 5
Color Your World!

Every hue throughout your work is altered by
every touch you add in other places.
~ Ruskin

Cozy, comfortable, elegant, masculine, sunny, bright, beautiful... every room is a statement! Much like the artist beginning a new painting, treat your walls like a canvas and begin to paint a picture with color first. Paint is the least expensive method to create the greatest change.

Where does it start? There's a method to the madness that everyone needs to understand to successfully create the feeling you want to project.

If you simply cannot imagine what color makes you feel good, walk around in stores, model homes and your friend's homes; pay attention to each room and how it 'feels' when you walk into the space.

Each design style has colors that specifically create the look and feel of that particular style. However, there are a multitude of shades of each of these colors, leaving you with the opportunity to personalize your design style to YOU.

Colors inspire feelings!

Walk into the rooms in your home and imagine how you want them to 'feel.' Then consider the following as you make the final selection. To sum it up:

Red

Physiological Effect: Red has been shown to increase blood pressure and stimulate the adrenal glands. The stimulation of the adrenals glands helps us become strong and increases our stamina. Pink, a lighter shade of red, helps muscles relax.

Psychological Effect: While red has proven to be a color of vitality and ambition it has been shown to be associated with anger. Sometimes red can be useful in dispelling negative thoughts, but it can also make one irritable. Pink has the opposite effect of red.

Pink induces feelings of calm, protection, warmth and nurturing. This color can be used to lessen irritation and aggression as it is connected with feelings of love. Red is sometimes associated with sexuality, whereas pink is associated with unselfish love.

Red is a highly energetic color. Take a look around fast food restaurants like McDonald's and you will frequently see reds and deep yellows. The subliminal message is 'hurry up and hurry out.' The more people they move, happily, through the restaurant the more they can serve.

If you are considering using red tones in your home keep in mind that it should be contained to a high energy area unless you have a careful plan to seduce your partner. We'll discuss that later in this book; the effects of colors, not seducing your partner!

Pink evokes a completely different feeling even though it is a shade of red. Little girls love it in every shade from Fuchsia to pale ice pink. It is a feel good, warm color. I try to avoid pinks or gender colors in master bedrooms.

Orange

Physiological Effect: Orange has proven to be a stimulus of the sexual organs. Also, it can be beneficial to the digestive system and can strengthen the immune system.

Psychological Effect: Orange has shown to have only positive effects on your emotional state. This color relieves feelings of self-pity, lack of self-worth and unwillingness to forgive. Orange opens your emotions and is a terrific antidepressant.

Orange is another high energy color. This color is sensual and sets a mood of sharing and playtime. The tangerine shades are warm and can be inviting in many areas. The deeper shades now available like the 'Olympic Grecian Leather' can actually set a sophisticated mood with white or light furniture.

Yellow

Physiological Effect: Yellow has proven to stimulate the brain. This stimulation can make you more alert and decisive. This color makes muscles more energetic and activates the lymph system.

Psychological Effect: Similarly to Orange, Yellow is a happy and uplifting color. It can also be associated with intellectual thinking: discernment, memory, clear thinking, decision-making and good judgment. Also affects aiding organization, understanding of different points of view.

Yellow builds self-confidence and encourages optimism. However, a dull yellow can bring on feelings of fear.

Yellow tends to work best in kitchens where a sunny wakeup call is inviting, in bathrooms to create a light hearted feeling and in children's playrooms.

This color energizes; you may want to reconsider a pure yellow in children's bedrooms for that very reason.

Gold Tones are popular shades that run from the palest gold tones to the deep gingerroot tones typically used to create a Mediterranean feel.

The soft tones are warm and relaxing, the deeper ones are more calming but all work well with darker furniture tones, metals and brown accessories.

In small rooms prepare to be overwhelmed by dark gold tones. The exception to this rule is using it in half baths where accessories can create an entirely different feeling.

Green

Physiological Effect: Green is said to be good for your heart. On a physical and emotional level, green helps your heart bring you physical equilibrium and relaxation. Green relaxes our muscles and helps us breathe deeper and slower.

Psychological Effect: Green creates feelings of comfort, laziness, relaxation and calmness. It helps us balance and soothe our emotions. Some attribute this to its connection with nature and our natural feelings of affiliation with the natural world when experiencing the color green.

Yet, **darker and grayer greens** can have the opposite effect. These olive green colors remind us of decay and death and can actually have a detrimental effect on physical and emotional health. Note that sickened cartoon characters always turn green.

Green is the comeback kid in colors. It has been widely used in those awful hospital rooms, avocado appliances we would rather forget and now in lime that makes an interesting, if faddish, statement.

Gray greens are very calming, allowing the accessories to make the statement and set the 'mood.'

Teals, or blue greens, lead us to a tropical paradise feeling if combined with accessories that complete that look. Think gentle ocean breezes or even tropical evening skies when considering this color.

Be careful when choosing the shade of teal for offices or places where you want to accomplish work tasks. You will probably not want to do it.

Blue

Physiological Effect: In contrast to red, blue proves to lower blood pressure. Blue can be linked to the throat and thyroid gland. Blue also has a very cooling and soothing affect, often making us calmer. Deep blue stimulates the pituitary gland, which then regulates our sleep patterns. This deeper blue also has proved to help the skeletal structure in keeping bone marrow healthy.

Psychological Effect: We usually associate the color blue with the night and thus we feel relaxed and calmed. Lighter blues make us feel quite and away from the rush of the day. These colors can be useful in eliminating insomnia. Like yellow, blue inspires mental control, clarity and creativity. However, too much dark blue can be depressing.

Blue is a love it or hate it color. In its palest shades it evokes calm and cool emotions.

Dark Blue, when combined with the right accessories, can be beautiful if the room is large enough to use this color for the 'canvas.' In master suites with all white accessories it becomes a paradise to relax in. Blue is the favorite color selection in all ethnic groups.

Purple

Physiological Effect: Violet has shown to alleviate conditions such as sunburn due to its purifying and antiseptic effect. This color also suppresses hunger and balances the body's metabolism. Indigo, a lighter purple, has been used by doctors in Texas as an anesthesia in minor operations because of its narcotic, 'a soothing or numbing agent affiliation.'

Psychological Effect: Purples have been used in the care of mental or nervous disorders because they have shown to help balance the mind and transform obsessions and fears. Indigo is often associated with the right side of the brain; stimulating intuition and imagination.

Violet is associated with bringing peace and combating shock and fear. Violet has a cleansing effect with emotional disturbances. Also, this color is related to sensitivity to beauty, high ideals and stimulates creativity, spirituality and compassion. Psychic power and protection has also been associated with violet.

Purple is a warm color that evokes a feeling of royalty, velvet, and beautiful sunsets. It is a balancing color that heals and yet stimulates creativity.

Brown

Psychological Effect: Brown is the color of the earth and ultimately home. This color brings feelings of stability and security. Sometimes brown can also be associated with withholding emotion and retreating from the world.

Psychological Effect: Brown is a bold color that makes a bold statement. It has a stabilizing effect; however, the way it is used will determine the actual affect. In large rooms with light wood or white trim it can create a warm and energizing feeling.

Beige, Taupe and light neutral shades of brown are a warmer shade of white. These colors make a perfect neutral backdrop and can feel warm or impersonal depending on the way you use furnishings and accessories.

If you are in doubt you will find that these colors or a very light brown/gray shade will match almost any furniture and set a neutral tone.

White

Psychological Effect: White is the color of ultimate purity. This color brings feelings of peace and comfort while it dispels shock and despair.

White can be used to give you a feeling of freedom and uncluttered openness. Too much white can give feelings of separation and can be cold and instill the feeling of isolation.

Show me a home or apartment with plain white walls, pictures hung high by the ceiling and furniture lined against the walls and I would like to introduce you to the 'House of Commons!'

White is cooling, calming and sometimes sophisticated; it can also feel cold, devoid of emotion and boring.

The same room transforms to sophisticated, soothing and beautiful when you add textured white window coverings, sumptuous white and contrasting rugs and throw pillows and a bold sofa. If this is combined with black and white photos you will feel like you have walked onto a movie set.

Be careful with a decision to paint everything white. Later we will talk about accessories and textures and how they affect your paint choice

Gray

Psychological Effect: Gray is the color of independence and self-reliance, although usually thought of as a negative color. It can be the color of evasion and non-commitment (since it is neither black nor white.) Gray indicates separation, lack of involvement and ultimately loneliness; unless…

Shades of Gray; Lighter shades of gray, with white tones, work perfectly with furniture that does not have browns as a primary color. This creates a soft and cool tone in the room.

Dark gray becomes a sophisticated backdrop when mixed with white or dark wood trim in the room.

Black is a bold, dramatic, confident and sophisticated color. It is a primary color and yet the attributes of both white and gray are felt in various shades of black. It is sometimes cold. Use it sparingly unless you have a serious plan for the entire room.

Everything is crystal clear now, right? It helps to envision the room bathed in your color selection. Close your eyes and 'feel' the room, visually place your favorite furniture or accessories in the space; then select the color that delivers the message you want to project.

Painting is a task that most people can perform at some level. If you are fortunate enough to be able to afford a painter you will likely make that choice.

Many painting contractors are looking for work since the housing and new construction market has become so depressed.

This means pricing is negotiable. Don't pass on this idea until you try pricing the job unless your budget does not accommodate the possibility.

If you intend to paint the rooms yourself (I always have) there are a few tips that will make your project run smoothly and produce results you can be proud of.

a) Choose a good, dependable paint. Satin or eggshell paint creates a soft and nearly flat appearance that does not show defects in the wall.

This happens because it has no sheen; light does not reflect off of it. Keep that in mind when choosing the color, you may want to slightly lighten the shade.

The washable flat paint also hides imperfections and works nicely with the Shabby Chic look. It is a little more expensive so weigh the benefits against the cost and then decide what works best for your budget.

b) Cover the floors, even if you think they are easy to clean or not really important. You'll be glad you did when clean up time is upon you.

c) If you are not completely comfortable with your trim brush, tape, tape and tape again.

d) Buy good paint rollers and the right length of roller covers. You really do get what you pay for in the paint materials.

e) Great brushes (horsehair if possible, with thin tapered edges) are the easiest to get a perfect edge on the trim work.

I was given the opportunity to learn from a professional and discovered that taking a long look at the angle of the wall and where it meets the ceiling is vital to know which way to set the brush on the wall and trim it out.

Stand back and take a good look at the angles of the walls and the ceiling and set the brush down with the bare tip of the brush at the point where the wall meets the ceiling.

f) Roll the walls in (W) patterns and back again. This is one time when straight lines will not be your friend. The more directions you roll in, the smoother the overall finish will be.

g) Use enamel paint on trim work. It wears beautifully and washes easily. It is also a pain to work with as it is almost never washable and turpentine will become a new friend.

h) I try to avoid semi gloss finishes. They are dated, show every imperfection on the walls and attract attention to the walls rather than letting them be the canvas they should be.

Who knew there was so much emotion in a simple can of paint? Make your selection and be brave; the results are so worth the effort.

If you are renting, get permission to paint and be prepared to repaint the walls to white when you leave.

I refuse to rent a property I cannot paint; I know it is essential to feeling like I am living in a home, not a house. Besides, however can we create a masterpiece if we have no canvas?

Painting Your Room

For step-by-step guides to painting your rooms I highly recommend going to your favorite search engine and selecting one of a host of available sites that provide written and video instructions.

The basic rules are light colors in rooms where the natural light is limited, thereby causing the room to feel dark when you enter it and light ceilings unless you have very high or vaulted ceilings. If you have chosen to paint your ceilings a different color, chose one this is a lighter shade of your original choice if you have low ceilings.

I have to add one more really neat tip I learned from a professional painter. I lived in a home with 19' ceilings; some were vaulted, some were trey. All seemed pretty daunting to me! I paid the painter for one room and learned very quickly the best tips I have ever been given.

Invest in the best paintbrush you can afford to buy. It should be very soft, horsehair if possible, thin and tapered at the tip and sturdy.

Trimming paint is all about the angle. Stand back for a moment and really look at the angle in the room.

You paint trim beginning from the back of the brush, allowing the tip of the brush (the pointed tapered end) to drag behind the paint stroke and fill in. The tip should find the 'bead' in the wall where the ceiling and wall come together.

Make SURE that you add the paint to the side of the brush that will be on the wall, wiping off excess paint on the opposite side of the brush.

Stand back once the paint is on the brush and look again at the ANGLE of the wall. Then, lay the paint brush flat against the wall, beginning at the back of the brush and drag along the line in a smooth motion.

I just finished painting the color 'Peppercorn' on a wall against a white ceiling and white baseboards with no taping or preparation and the line is perfect – simply by using this method! Try it first; it is a time saver and money saver.

Painting Your Floors

This is a very simple procedure to complete; however, the most important issue with painting floors is making the determination that the floor is suitable for painting and if not, what you need to do to prepare it before you start. It must be smooth and moisture free. Wood floors can be sanded and any spaces filled in with wood filler. Concrete must be free of cracks or blemished or be repaired to have a smooth working surface.

Once your floor is properly prepared you will need to select your color and ask your paint supplier to mix it from the floor painting bases. It is applied with a roller using an extension. Two coats is the minimal you will want to apply. Then finish with poly to protect the paint and give the floor a lasting sheen.

The internet is a wonderful place to learn anything today. Go back to your favorite search engine and find the particular problem you are facing. You will be sure to find detailed instructions and probably even videos to walk you through the process.

Wallpaper Instructions

Wallpapering a wall or a room may feel a little scary if you've never attempted it.

The good news is that it is a fairly simple process. Just as in painting a wall, preparing the surface is the most is very important first step. If your walls are not smooth this will be obvious even with the wallpaper.

You will need to patch and sand any holes or cracks on the surface. If your walls have really obvious defects you can sand the area first and cut a piece of a brown paper bag to cover the area; use your wallpaper glue to attach the paper to the wall. Press it firmly into place and smooth out the wrinkles and let it dry. You will have a smooth surface that easily covers with the new paper.

For detailed instructions pick a good search engine and review the written instructions and the videos available online.

Chapter 6
Looking Into You

You guessed it; it's time for windows and how to treat them to compliment your plan.

You can create the design style you have chosen; however, the windows are important to arrive at creating the look you are planning.

Take a good look at your windows and the placement of them. This is the not the time to decide whether they need replaced; we simply want to use them to the best advantage for your design style. Windows are square, paned, arched, long and narrow, wide and short, they come in a multitude of sizes and shapes.

Regardless of your window style, we need to get to know them.

Examples of window styles:
High/short/narrow

Dormer style
High and arched window
Long and narrow window
Abundance of narrow windows
Paned bay window
A 'glasshouse' effect from windows
Excess of glass, French doors and windows
High, arched windows
Cornered windows
High, narrow arched windows
Original bay window style with seating
Round room with a wall of windows
Tall narrow windows with arch above
High, standard square windows
Sliding glass doors take the place of windows

Even if your windows look different than these pictures, your style is represented here. Arches placed above windows create and arched in appearance in a typical are window.

Window panes are a part of the construction in older windows; if you don't like them you have a few choices. You can use a window treatment that obscures the design or replace them.

The newer paned windows are strips that will snap out and give you a clean un-obscured window if that look is attractive to you.

This book is not about replacing windows but that is an option if you desire to do so! We are going to work with what we have.

Some window styles reflect the style of the home. For instance, a home with arched windows may be somewhat of a challenge when creating a Primitive Design. Still, we can do that. Just keep reading!

Likewise, the older more typical square windows challenge the Contemporary, Spanish and Southwestern designs.

Once you have selected your style, paint colors and floor treatment, the windows complete your canvas. The picture will be complete when the room is finished!

Tips to begin:

a) Wash the windows!

b) Clean the woodwork and paint if necessary.

c) Assess the challenge! Do the size and style of the windows work as they are, or do you need to change the perception to create your style?

d) Get creative; packaged window treatments are made for the 'house of commons,' not your palace! When creating your own design, you become the leader, not the follower.

e) Measure the actual windows both vertical and horizontal; then measure from the top of the wall to the floor.

f) Take a moment and caulk your windows. Heat and air conditioning is lost through windows and doors, increasing your energy bills and making it harder to heat or cool your home. Caulking also prevents ants and other undesirables from entering your home.

g) If you live in a manufactured house, tear down those 'made for a trailer' window treatments! Nothing says I'm perched on wheels like the little valances and kitchen curtains hanging all over the house. You will be amazed at how your home can look!

Now we're ready to begin! Let's look at materials, and what is possible.

If you are working with Southwestern, Spanish or Primitive designs, regardless of whether you have square, arched or small windows; try picking up full length wood bi-fold doors and painting them or grab a can of Min Wax spray stain and put the finish of your choice on the doors. They fold out just like shutters and can be used on sliders as well as windows.

For very little money you have custom window treatments!

Cottage designs work great with the plantation shutter styles. You can hang these higher and wider that the actual window if you need to visually increase the size of the window to make a bigger statement.

Give some thought to hand railing for stairs and how they can work as curtain rods! These come in nearly every style, some with intricate design in addition to the more typical styles.

Mediterranean and Spanish styles can use wrought iron pieces to create interesting rods.

All of these items can be picked up at the same thrift stores, consignment stores, Craig's List and any other source you know would be worth looking at in your area.

We're creating a masterpiece here and can hardly be bothered to simply pick up a simple rod and hang it up. Window design starts from the rods.

If your home has small, older windows try hanging your drapes from the top of the wall and extend them out past the actual window. Visually the wall and the windows appear larger; and the room feels more substantial. This is also a good trick to eliminate the arches if your design is more suited to a straight line in the windows.

Drop in at the remnant section of the fabric store. Look for large bolts that are offered at $1.00 a yard. You're looking for texture that will compliment your personal style.

If you're not handy with a sewing machine, never fear; just purchase Stitch Witchery and head for your ironing board to create rod pockets at the top and finished hems at the bottom.

Curtains that pool onto the floor are much more appealing and do not look like pre-packaged curtains.

Look at sheets if you do not want to spend time at the fabric store. They are long, offered in a wide range of colors and already have top and bottom hems.

Just slit the sides of the top hem and insert the rod after using your stitch witchery magic or hand needle and thread to complete the newly cut seam.

Sheets work great as shower curtains on spring rods; insert a liner behind it and decorate away!

If you plan to tie your curtains back look at wide cloth ribbon and other trims that are not so fussy and do not appear prepackaged.

If you are working with a Victorian, Classic or Traditional design look at the long table cloths that also offer special designs particular to your style. Try adding long strings of pearls that are found in craft stores and Christmas decorations. They make fabulous trims!

Natural hemp ropes work perfectly as tiebacks for Cottage (especially Seaside Cottage designs) Country and Primitive.

Look for natural fabrics like unbleached muslin to bring a true country or Primitive feeling into the space.

If you have typical windows and are looking for a whole new look with an unconditional fix;

define your style and consider adding plantation shutters that are 18" shy of the top of the window.

Next, look for leaded glass or, designed to mimic lead stained Plexiglas sections; place this section above the shutter to cover the rest of the window and add a trim board. Suddenly your 'same old windows' now feature leaded glass and thick, rich wood shutters. Stain or paint the shutters to match your design plan.

You no longer have average or typical windows. It's a brand new view!

Avoid those 'found in every home' mini blinds if possible. They feel like a cheap fix, and are unbecoming to a palace and your plan. Dare to be different.

The 'fan' treatment for the top of arched windows needs to head to the curb too. The arches grace the top of the window; leave them bare and let the sun shine in!

Part of your plan is to make your home different and spectacular; affordably!

Make a real effort to think outside the traditional prepackaged window treatments available almost everywhere. Search for great deals on things that can be repurposed into your plan.

For the classic window covering look, nothing compares to custom fabric drapes and curtains. The simplicity of hanging drapery adds elegance and sophistication to your dining room, living room, or bedroom. Drapes hang from above the window down to the floor, hanging on either a rod or with pins and a pin knuckle for easy sliding. And because custom drapes are long and made of fabric, you can get them in just about any color you can imagine. Not only do they give your rooms a classy look, they can also be matched to your decor easily and precisely.

Pleats or No Pleats?

Pleated drapes are designed to create a consistent pleated look starting at the top where the gathers form. The drapes then hang in lines, giving a long, tall look to any room. With pins and a pin knuckle, you'll find that pleated drapes look perfect all the time. The shape and frequency of the pleats will be consistent, no matter whether the drapes are open or closed.

Drapes that don't have pleats will have a flat and straight look with wider folds when the drapes are pulled closed. Flat drapes are usually hung on a bar, either with large grommet holes or with simple fabric loops. Un-pleated custom drapes look great in dark colors, such as you might want in your bedroom or entertainment den.

Colors, Stripes and Solids

Custom drapes come in a wide assortment of colors, including stripes, solids, and even textures like linen and a crushed look that is very modern and stylish. A slight woven look or a very flat look is also possible. This means that you can match your colors as well as an appropriate texture to your rooms.

Pairs or Singles?

You can also get long, custom curtains in a pair, so that the two curtains move to opposite sides of your windows or doors, or you can get a single curtain that is always held to one side or the other. Either look will still give you the elegance of custom drapery.

Lining Options

Some drapes do not require lining to block the light. But if you want something lightweight with a liner, you also have the option of pleated or not pleated liners, which will aid in darkening the room and keeping the ambient temperature even.

Window Treatments

Choose the Perfect Window Treatments

Long Panes

Bare windows are rarely the best choice when decorating a room. Window treatments--whether piped, pleated, puddled, or plain--add fluidity and softness to a room's hard edges. And in terms of practicality, they add privacy and light control. They also can help conceal a room's flaws or accentuate its charms.

Three of design's heavy hitters--fabric, texture, and pattern--come into play when you're selecting the perfect treatment. But choosing the type of treatment your room needs is the first order of business. We've made it easy: These timeless treatments will inspire and guide you through the looks that stylish windows are wearing.

Puddled Curtains

Puddled curtains are an exception to the "just touching the floor." rule. Puddled curtains are several inches too long. Puddled curtains have a luxurious look that is often preferred by homeowners who have formally decorated and furnished homes. Puddled curtains work best when they are stationary, meaning that you do not need to open and close them often. They also look best when they are made from luxurious fabrics and are placed in formal settings.

Custom formal puddle drapes
Goblet Puddle
Puddled Ring Curtains
French Puddled Curtains

Valances
A valance is a little bit of fabric that does a big job. It hangs across the top of a window, adding softness, color, and pattern to a hard architectural element. Purely decorative, a valance helps establish a room's style. At its most basic, a slip of fabric can be attached to a rod with clip rings. For more detail, add pinch pleats.

The simple valance is a casual treatment that works well for family areas such as the kitchen, breakfast room, and bathroom. In rooms where privacy isn't an issue, the valance can hang alone. When privacy is a concern, the valance easily pairs with a hard treatment, such as a blind, shade, or shutters.

Ringed Valance and Box-Pleated Valances
If you appreciate a classic decorating style will fall in love with the box-pleated valance. This tailored treatment is a natural in rooms where you want a formal air, such as a living room, dining room, or

master bedroom. The stationary treatment's crisp stitched pleats lie flat against a mounting board, which is typically attached to the wall with simple L-shape brackets.

The box-pleated design is easily duplicated on furnishings such as table coverings, slipcovers, or bed skirts to unify a room. Here, fabric-covered buttons accent the corner pleats on the table topper to mimic the valance.

Simple Swags

Sometimes a simply knotted scarf worn around the neck is the perfect accent for an outfit. A simple swag on a window dresses up a room the same way. A loosely slung fabric strip, unlined or lined, draped over a decorative rod or wound over a tieback at each top corner of a window frame can add an abundance of style. The middle of the fabric strip acts as a valance; the ends, whether cut into opposing diagonals or simply hemmed, softly hang down the sides of the window.

Swags can be made of luxurious fabrics to fit formal decor or dressed down in cottons befitting a cottage or country home. The beauty of this style is its simplicity, so it's most appropriate used alone on windows where privacy is not an issue.

Balloon Shades

For the ultimate romantic gesture, nothing beats a billowy balloon shade. This sumptuous fabric shade features cascading scallops that culminate in graceful, blousy folds along the bottom. Cords strung though rings on the back make the shade movable, and as the treatment is raised, the vertical gathers create dramatic poufs. Because this treatment usually remains raised, it acts as a valance more often than a shade. The amount of fabric used--at least twice the width of the window--creates the opulent look. Large designs can get lost in the multiple gathers, so opt for solid-color or small-pattern fabrics. Be aware, too, that the number of gathers, pleats, or scallops creates different looks within the balloon-shade and valance family. An Austrian shade, for example, has less shirring and is therefore more tailored than its cousin, the balloon shade. Because this window treatment is so showy, use it in small doses.

Pleated Balloon Shade and Tie-Up Shade

Simplicity is the name of the game with tie-up shades. Sometimes called a stagecoach-style shade, this economical treatment uses fabric in its most unconstructed form: It hangs flat from a rod or mounting board, and then the bottom edge is hand-rolled or folded to the desired position. Fabric ties, ribbons, or cords hold the rolls or folds in place. Adjusting the shade requires untying and rerolling it by hand, making this treatment more decorative than functional. Consider using it where you're likely to leave the shade down to hide an unsightly view or open in a room where privacy or sunlight isn't an issue.

Tie-up Shade Tips

Because so much of the fabric is visible, a tie-up shade offers a good opportunity to use a large-scale pattern. Just make sure the fabric keeps its shape when rolled. Or add bulk by lining a lightweight fabric to give the shade a finished look when rolled up. For tidy rolls, sew a dowel into the bottom hem. This treatment's simple styling makes it a natural for casual decorating schemes, but it also can be a welcome change of pace in formal rooms.

Roman Shades

For the look of luxury without yards of flowing fabric, a Roman shade is a wise choice. When closed, the shade is a flat fabric panel. When raised, cascades of deep, horizontal folds are responsible for the tidy look. Cords strung through rings on the back of the fabric give the shade its mobility. Some Roman shades are made without dowels or lining, resulting in looser, puffier folds.

Roman Shade Tips

A Roman shade can be mounted inside or outside a window frame. Though the shade is often used alone, it can be the practical layer combined with side panels or a valance. Appropriate almost anywhere, a Roman shade's level of formality is defined by fabric and trim choices. You could use plain muslin in a sunroom or toile in a master bedroom. Just be sure to choose fabric that can form handsome folds.

Cornices

Thinking of a cornice as a wood valance, it is typically made from plywood, assembled with wood screws and corner brackets, then painted or covered with wallpaper or fabric and mounted to the wall above a window. Like a valance, a cornice can appear alone or team with another treatment. Because it is usually made of wood, a cornice benefits from being paired with a soft treatment, such as a curtain or fabric shade, to temper its hard lines.

These structural lines are especially effective in rooms that lack interesting architecture. They can camouflage a window's wimpy trim or bring interest to a room that doesn't have crown moldings.

Rod-Pocket Drapes

Of the many ways to attach a drapery panel to a rod, few match the ease of the rod pocket. In this treatment, the curtain rod simply slips through a channel sewn into the panel's top edge. The tighter the fit, the more dramatic the shirring. For a ruffled header, sew a pocket a few inches down from the top edge; when the rod is pushed through, the fabric above it fans out to form a ruffle.

Rod-pocket panels are commonly made of lightweight fabrics and left unlined for a casual look. But don't overlook this style for more formal decor. For a sumptuous style statement, consider plush velvet panels shirred tightly on a substantial rod. Because panels don't slide easily on a rod, especially when tightly gathered, they're typically used in the closed position or held open with decorative tiebacks.

Panels with Rings

Prickly metal hooks used to be standard fare for hanging draperies. Stuck into the back of a panel, the hardware was out of sight and out of mind. No more. Wood or metal rings that slide along a pole allow you to put hardware in a starring role, complementing virtually any style of drapery. Besides being fashionable, panels with rings are easy to open and close and offer an alternative to anyone who dislikes the cord-and-pulley system of traverse rods.

Tips for Using Panels with Rings

When using accessories to hang drapes or curtains think of rings, rods, brackets, and finials as a drapery's jewelry. Hardware with unusual shapes, eye-catching colors, or high contrast will draw the eye up, focusing attention on the top of the panels, window, and ceiling. Large rings can be hand-tacked along a panel's top edge; small clip-on rings are fine for suspending lightweight fabrics. Some rings open and can slip through buttonholes or grommets at the top of the panel.

Pinch Pleated with Rings and Pleated Panels

In the world of window treatments, pleated drapery panels are the classics. They withstand the whims of window fashion, adding elegance and sophistication to any room. There are several styles of pleats, all of which are sewn into a panel's top edge to create a decorative header. Pleats are often formed with the help of header tape, which is available by the yard at fabrics stores. Sewn to the panel's back, the tape forms pleats when pulled. Hooks are then inserted into the tape and hung on rings, or more typically traverse rods, which have a cord-and-pulley system for opening and closing the panels.

Standard Pleated Panels and Pleat Styles

The most common pleat, the pinch pleat is a series of equally spaced single, double, or triple pleats that are pinched in the center, forming fans above and below the pinch.

A goblet pleat is similar to a triple-pinch pleat, except the pleating above the pinch is exaggerated with a stiffening card or paper to form a wineglass silhouette.

Pencil pleats are narrow single pleats formed in neat, tight folds.

Cartridge pleats are also single pleats, but they are spaced more widely and the tops rounded.

Tuscan Pleats

Tab-Top Panels

The natural and casual elegance of tab-top panels makes them a natural for country and cottage decorating. There are many variations, but standard tabs are simply loops of fabric sewn into or onto the valance's top seam. The panel hangs relatively flat from these tabs, providing a good opportunity to showcase interesting fabric prints.

Because the curtain rod is visible between the tabs, you can add decorative rods and finials for more impact. To maintain the fuss-free feel this style evokes, use cotton or linen fabrics in simple checks, stripes, plaids, or floral designs. These are usually stationary panels, because drawing them across the rod can be cumbersome.

Tab Top Panels and Shutters
Wood Plantation Shutters Add Enduring, Classic Beauty to Your Home

The most desired of all window coverings are real wood shutters. A classic window covering choice, they exude a sense of permanence, so every time you see them, you know that you are indeed home.

Real wood shutters are made from 100% North American Hardwoods, which have been harvested from certified forests. Shutters are available in a variety of finishes to complement your decor. Slat sizes are also a matter of choice. Choose from 2" slats, 3" slats or view-preserving 4" slats.

Curtain and Drapery Lengths

Floor Length Curtains Just as pants that are several inches too short are unflattering and distracting, so are curtains that are too short. Curtains that hang about 1/8 to 1/4 inch above the floor, just touch the floor or have a slight break look neat and professional. Decorators often hang curtains so that they are as close to the ceiling as possible, to make windows and ceilings look taller. This is good advice, so do hang your curtains as high as possible, but not so high that they do not touch the floor.

Puddled Curtains

Puddled curtains are an exception to the "just touching the floor rule. Puddled curtains are several inches too long. Puddled curtains have a luxurious look that is often preferred by homeowners who have formally decorated and furnished homes. Puddled curtains work best when they are stationary, meaning that you do not need to open and close them often. They also look best when they are made from luxurious fabrics and are placed in formal settings.

Window-length Curtains   You may choose to dress shorter windows with shorter curtains. Short windows that do not extend close to the floor are often found in bathrooms and kitchens. If your window is closer to the ceiling than the floor, it can look awkward to have floor-length curtains. Instead, hang or hem your curtains so that the bottom of the panel is either just touching the window sill, or hanging to the bottom of the trim underneath the window.

Standard Ready-made Curtain Lengths

The height of your home's ceilings often determines the length of your curtain panels, as builders usually install taller windows in homes with higher ceilings. Ready-made curtains generally come in standard lengths: 84 inches for 8-foot ceilings, 96 inches for 9-foot ceilings and 108 inches for 10-foot ceilings. If you like to puddle your curtains, simply buy one size up. You can sometimes find curtains that are 120 inches long; these work well for puddling curtains in a home with 10-foot ceilings.

Other Considerations
Before hanging your ready-made curtains, always measure them first. Dimensions listed on the curtain packages are approximate, and the actual curtain may be slightly longer or shorter than the package states. Take any curtain rings or headers into consideration, as these can add or take length away from curtain measurements.

Chapter 7
Into Your Light

'Light always follows the path of the beautiful.'
~ Unknown

What's YOUR style? You are likely to find it in your lighting selections! This may surprise you but; the light choices you make typically define your style.

Lighting is everything! Choose wisely and you will be well on your way to creating YOUR space. If you are uncertain as to what your style actually is take a look at the lighting examples in this chapter.

Notice what you are drawn to and then explore that look. You will probably find that some of your furniture pieces will work nicely to create that style, the other pieces we will work on!

If you discover that you are drawn to a particular style of lighting, you will probably discover that is your style!

Some are combined styles that work well together to create a specific look and feel.

Great lighting is found in yard sales, online stores, (Overstocked.com is a good one) eBay, and on Craig's List (many contractors sell lighting that customers rejected on Craig's List), in the newspaper, at thrift stores and, especially at the Habitat for Humanity Thrift Store!

Habitat for Humanity has been very blessed to receive donations from Lowes, Home Depot and a host of other large companies. If you have one locally, find it and bookmark it in your mind!

At the end of this chapter you will find detailed instructions on installing your lighting. If you are not comfortable with doing this job, look in the newspaper, on Craig's List or a weekly paper that has Handyman advertisements or ask a neighbor or relative to do this.

The job is relatively simple so long as you are simply replacing a fixture. On the other hand, if you are relocating electrical fixtures, call a licensed electrician to complete this for you. This is an added expense and we will explore ways to sue what you have and work from that point.

Define Your Style!

Art Deco Lighting

Classical Lighting

Contemporary Lighting

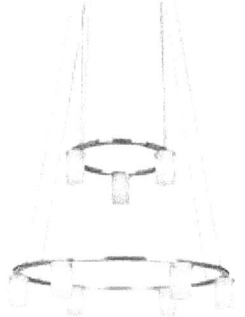

Country Lighting

Country Cottage Lighting

Eclectic Lighting

French Country Lighting

Mediterranean Lighting

Minimalist Lighting

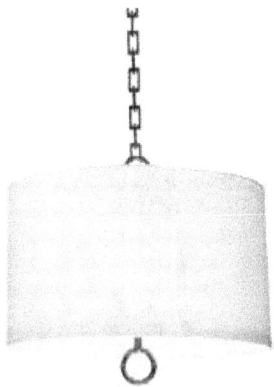

Modern Lighting

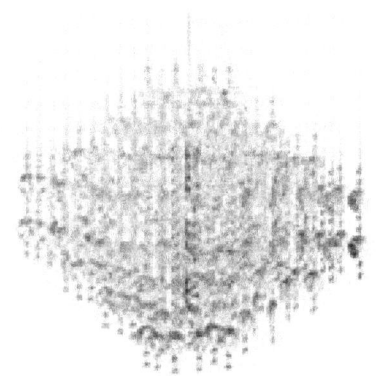

Oriental Lighting

Primitive Lighting

Rustic Lighting

Retro Lighting

Seaside Cottage Lighting

Shabby Chic Lighting

Southwestern Lighting

Spanish Lighting

Traditional Lighting

Tuscan Lighting

Victorian Lighting

Whimsical Lighting

If you take a moment to carefully review the styles you will notice that each has lines, shapes and detail that are particular to the style.

Find the one that you like the most things about the look and feel, imagine them in your own home and you will have defined your own personal style!

Some tips about lighting your palace:

1) Entry areas greet everyone; choose a size in your style that is befitting of the greeting and the size of the area you are defining.

2) Long entry halls may require a larger light and wall sconces or an entry table with lamps to properly light the area.

3) Don't select long, pendant lighting for the entry if you have 8' ceilings. You can do this in the dining area because the table is placed under the lighting and no one is walking in the area.

4) Grand foyers deserve a grand light! Go big or go home.

5) Wall sconces around mirrors in bath areas are welcoming and provided necessary dressing light.

6) Choose your dining room light in proportion with the size of your table. Don't be afraid to drop it lower than what you might think is typical. Lighting makes a statement! If you want it to be intimate lighting you have to set the stage with furniture and accessories and say it with light!

7) Avoid fans on dining room lighting unless you want to create a very informal space. It also cools the food on the table and stirs dust above and onto the food.

8) Ceiling fans are a must in some areas; although some decorators rush to remove them, others will scurry to install them! If you determine that a ceiling fan must be in your bedrooms, avoid the inexpensive (and cheap looking) light kits; opt for nice lamps and a decorative fan that matches the room decor.

9) If you have a budget that permits you to shop for quality fans with lighting that makes a difference in the room, go for it!

10) Breakfast bars in kitchens become a special place if they are defined with two or three pendant lights.

11) Hall lighting is largely ignored, yet it is typically a long area that leads to probably half of

your home. Use that opportunity to make a special statement!

Track lighting is now available in attractive styles that fit any décor. You may want to look at those as an option, or, supplement your overhead lights with wall sconces.

We are now ready for the final piece in building your canvas, the flooring. Detailed step-by-step instructions with illustrations are included in the next chapter.

Then comes the really fun part... the furniture; you are about to become a creative giant!

Chapter 8
Ushering In Your Luck

"Opportunity dances with those already on the dance floor."

~ H. Jackson Brown Jr.

Floors are important! They are a roadway that carries the traffic through your home. Who knew!

After spending all that time on painting and properly defining your home with perfect lighting; there's the same old floor! Now what?

I think energy is very important in our lives. We can 'feel' it but may not be aware of how it affects us. Because of that, I have included the following Feng Shui information on flooring.

Feng Shui is not just about building structures that are supposed to usher in "luck"; they encompass a lot more than that. Both Feng Shui and Vaastu, the Indian art of placement, focus on positioning, planning and orienting not just the structure but also the furnishings to offer greater support to the occupants. It addresses the energy around the occupants, its cause and effect, and the effect of the immediate surroundings.

Ensuring that your home is in harmony with nature and your immediate environment will affect every person who enters your home is a positive way.

Every day we encounter energy imbalances when we are subjected to energy fields like, solar energy fields due to movement of sun, geo-magnetic fields due to the magnetic field interaction and rotation of the earth and thermal imbalance due to temperature changes.

Typically, one side of a house is subjected to intense solar radiation, while the other side remains in the shadow region. This creates an energy imbalance around the house and flows through to the interior and the occupants.

The greater the imbalance, the more intense its effect on the occupants; this kind of imbalance distorted energy fields as these fields begin to resonate to give rise to hazardous levels of radiation which affect the occupants of the home.

Ignoring this will interrupt the smooth flow of energy in and around your home. Learning the principals of Feng Shui will help to restore the imbalance or equalizing the thermal difference.

Some excellent ideas to remember as you correct energy imbalance in your home are:

- More open spaces in the North and East direction.
- Solid walls and no openings on the South side.
- Adding more greenery or trees in the South to have a humid environment.
- But, most importantly, choose good flooring.

The flooring in a building not only breathes life in terms of décor and aesthetics but also defines how the energy flows there and through the space.

You can control the atmosphere of your house or apartment. Big surface areas such as flooring will have the greatest influence, and it is worth taking great care over the materials you use.

Natural materials create the best energy flow. These include wood, brick marble, granite and slate. Marble has never been out of fashion and is available in a variety of colors. Bricks are available in different shades of red and orange can also be used as ethnic flooring. Bamboo flooring has recently become very fashionable and is eco friendly because it reproduces so quickly.

Natural materials tend to carry the energy more easily than synthetic materials.

A rough textured surface (such as a wool carpet) slows down chi, making it more yin. Hard or shiny surfaces (such as ceramic tiles) speed up the flow of chi, creating a more yang atmosphere. By incorporating these guidelines into your flooring plan you are able to harmonize the energy in the room and around your family and guests.

Every natural material enhances a specific flow of chi; applying the simplicity of the eight directions; you can determine which materials are best suited to each area of your home.

Using specific materials will lead to a more harmonious exchange of chi and develop distinct atmospheres in each part of your home. Review the list below and apply the ideas to your home and the atmosphere and energy flow you wish to create.

• White marble which enhances positive energy and reflects and polarizes sunlight well in the Northeast sector.

• Shades of yellow, like the popular Southwest Indian Yellows towards the Southwest promote good energy flow. The Southwest is designated the negative energy corner so brighter colors that anchor the space and create a 'heavy' energy attraction correct this.

• The Northwest sections of your home are influenced by wind energy. Choose blues, whites, silvers and creams that reflect the flow of the wind.

• The southeast corner of your home will do well with reds and oranges in some shade that fits your color plan.

Floors will shout or whisper, depending on how you treat them. Some styles seem to feel like they must be defined by specific flooring. That is the shouting method!

If your floors do not 'match' your idea of the design you are creating you have a few choices to make them whisper so the bulk of your masterpiece will shout.

If you live in an apartment or a rental home you may think you are stuck with your floors; take heart.

Solutions for shouters:

Cover the floor! That's right; cover it with something that ties it to the style you are creating. Even if the floor has carpet, cover it with a large room size rug or one that leaves only a border of the original color, if there is anything you like about it.

I urge you to check out Flea Markets, Thrift Stores, Consignment Stores, Craig's List and Overstocked.com to find a rug that will make the cut.

b) Select the very inexpensive woven mats to create an oriental feeling in the space.

c) Tile and carpet squares are sold by the box pretty inexpensively. Find the nap and color that you work for your idea and put them in place.

d) If you own your home, have carpet and cannot afford to replace it with anything; take it up and paint the subflooring! It works great with rugs to complete the design.

e) If you have wood floors that are the wrong color or in a bad state of repair; make the repairs and rent a floor sander.

Sanding is a fairly easy job that provides you with a clean slate. Then select the stain that makes you want to shout about it!

f) Barter the work with someone who has materials and experience.

g) Create visual points to break an open floor plan by changing the flooring. In very open plans the entry can break away from tile or something durable to wood or carpet in the actual living space, thereby creating a defined space without walls.

h) Avoid the 'checkerboard' floor syndrome. Breaking the flooring is fine for obvious areas like entry's, kitchens, baths and lanais. A different floor color or style in every room dates your home and makes it look and feel choppy and smaller.

When flooring changes design, color or material in every room you will soon begin to feel like you've been check-mated instead of mated with your dream home!

Kicking your old floor to the curb?

Consider other options. If you have always wanted wood floors and they are not practical for your home or location; search out the new tile selections.

'Looks like wood' tile floors

Tile manufactures have listened to their buying audience and created beautiful tiles that look like wood. It is easy care, scuff proof and humidity does not affect its performance.

Save diagonal ceramic or marble tile jobs for large rooms. While they are beautiful, they also attract attention to the floor space and make the room appear smaller.

Select light tile colors to make your room appear larger. Larger tile sizes also make the room appear more spacious.

Pergo or other manufactured wood flooring is far less expensive but also, far less durable. It is manmade wood and a little easier to install but have a care here, if it is not properly adhered to the subflooring, it 'bounces' when you walk across it and screams 'thrift.'

Real hard wood is more expensive but if time is on your side you can watch for the spring specials and the dead of winter liquidation of these materials.

Carpeting is still considered a good option for bedrooms and upper levels. It is available in a multitude of styles, naps, colors and designs.

Unless you plan to live forever in your home, or don't mind repainting later, avoid fads and colors that you will tire of. Select colors that you can interchange accessories with to create a new look and feel later.

The general rule with carpeting is Berbers are more durable, neutrals are preferable.

Lose the notion that a carpeted kitchen, bath or dining room is a good idea. Most people prefer to be able to easily clean the surfaces of these areas.

In homes that offer large, separate dining areas this rule can be bent; personally, I'd rather not; opt for wood or tile.

When you begin to install flooring, doors, hardware or plumbing you must decide whether you are handy and want to learn or tackle these tasks alone or, whether it is time to search the kingdom for qualified and affordable assistance.

If so, head to the 'Know When to Fold Em' chapter and review the section about contractors and subs. This is an area where cutting corners has definite rules of procedure. What's it all about? It is about doing what you can, where you can to claim your space and make it work for you!

Chapter 9
A Change is Gonna Come!

By now you're probably thinking, "Good luck with that change thing."

A lot of topics have been covered in the process of building your 'canvas. It is an important process, necessary to determine exactly what you want to create and which of the ideas fit into your budget and final plan for the space you want to transform. In later chapters we will review different rooms in the home and how these ideas can work, very affordably, to create a stunning completed project.

For now, it is time to take a look at how to make it happen. Pictures may speak a thousand words but directions make it a lot easier to arrive at your destination.

Beginning with the Sophisticated Classic design style we will walk through how to transform a space that is diametrically opposite to that style and then one that is perfect for that style. To share ideas in a graphic manner each style will be addressed in this chapter, including furniture pieces that will work and how to re-purpose them to fit the plan.

Sophisticated Classic

Remember this design style? It is sumptuous and glitzy while maintaining a comfortable ambience.

This style is an elegant blend of refined traditional furniture, jewelry-like accessories, and pale hues. Patrician old-world elements pair with cleaner Art Deco shapes. The look evokes a more formal lifestyle. When defining Sophisticated Classic, think Grace Kelly, Tiffany & Co., and Charlotte from Sex and the City when defining this style.

Features:

Delicate furniture pieces with feminine lines and tapered legs define this style. A palette of neutrals and soft colors, grand chandeliers, luxurious fabrics, like silk and velvet, rich dark woods with polished veneers are perfect additions. Deluxe accent materials, including metal, marble, glass and symmetrical floor plans are typical to this style

Notice that the room pictured has high ceilings and lots of tall windows, crown molding and canister lights for drama. If you have a room that looks like this one:

The challenges are not so difficult to overcome. This room features 12' ceilings, walls of windows and is already a very sophisticated setting. By simply adding an upper trim to the baseboards and adding crown moldings to the top of the wall you will have made a good start on the initial staging. The floors are marble which work nicely with this style; adding large rugs, preferably with a very high nap in dramatic complimentary colors will complete the floor changes. Canister lights are already installed. You need only to add a very ornate chandelier to the room and the basic lighting is completed.

This room provides sufficient natural lighting to permit adding deep colors of wallpaper or paint, creating the drama you will need to compliment this style. Draping all of the windows in the long drapery or custom puddled styles shown below will complete the window treatments.

What if you are working with this room?
A little tougher, huh!

We have low ceilings in this older home, natural hardwood flooring, short windows that limit the natural light and a *radiator* heating system!

What is not readily noticeable is the wide baseboards and window trim that can easily become sophisticated, again. When this home was constructed, it was exactly that!

Wallpapering this entire room will overwhelm the room and the occupants. You will have the same result if you paint all the walls in a dark color or apply dramatic wallpaper to all the walls. We are looking for quiet elegance in this room to arrive at the sophisticated classic style.

The woodwork will work best in a pure white color; all of it. The walls will work better in a light silvery, opal or pearl white shade. The bay window area can be wallpapered with a white background and a darker silver flocked design as shown.

The puddled custom drape will tie the natural architecture in this room to the new look you want to create. Hang them at the very top of wall, just below the ceiling. I have had several really good experiences with using king size sheets for this look. They are inexpensive and available in many thrift stores at great prices. Satin ribbon works perfect for the ties.

If your budget is tight you can leave the floors as they are and simply add large rugs in very dramatic colors that work with the accessories you choose. Rungs are making a statement in this room so I strongly advise you look for long naps or a look that feels sumptuous.

The ceiling in this room is low and not really

open to a chandelier unless it is directly over the bed or in the seating area. It will be uncomfortable to walk through the room if is located in the traffic pattern. Consider looking for Chrystal or silver extravagant lamps. You can also find these in thrift stores and new online at several stores.

Budget permitting, you can sand the floors and apply white bone to the floors. You will have a quietly elegant, beautiful floor to complete this look.

If you are not limited in funds to furnish the room, this is your goal:

Search for delicate furniture pieces with feminine lines and tapered legs; a palette of neutrals and soft colors, grand chandeliers, luxurious fabrics, like silk and velvet, and rich dark woods with polished veneers. Deluxe accent materials, including metal, marble, glass and symmetrical floor plans are typical to this style.

If you are limited in funds and willing to work on your furniture pieces, this is for you! Let's assume that you have a typical square style and wood tones on your dresser or the primary pieces in the room. How could this possibly work? Silver is a necessary accent in this design style. There are many websites available that will provide detailed instructions on how paint your furniture with very exotic paint colors that are pricy. Take a look at this piece:

This is a very old buffet picked up at an auction for a ridiculous low price. It was scratched mahogany and in poor condition.

The owner used spray on paint remover, let it dry, lightly sanded the piece and then painted three coats of silver fence paint (very inexpensive) to create this beautiful piece! A single coat of poly and a change of hardware, also pre-owned and therefore very inexpensive, and this beautiful piece emerged! The top was lightly sanded and a coat of mahogany Minwax and poly was applied to complete the piece. At the end of this chapter detailed instructions on how to refinish furniture is available.

Tables do not need to match in design. Combing round tables with square pieces adds interest to the room. This table was picked up off the street, left for the trash pickup when someone moved. I could hardly leave it just sitting there! It has great bones but the finish was almost completely gone.

It was sanded lightly and painted in a bright red color. The 'wood grain' was brushed on with stain and then wiped off to create the 'wood grain' look. Poly was applied as a finish to the table and hardware was changed out to match the silver piece we just reviewed. This particular room was finished in red and gray tones. Notice the dark coffee table that blends with the top of the first silver piece; and the red shades that were added to existing, older lamps. This is a very dramatic completion of a room that was originally finished very traditionally with browns and greens prior to this transformation!

I have included the 'Barely Get Along Street Rocks!' chapter from the original 'Make It Mine' book in this book to assist you in locating the best possible prices on the furnishings and accessories that you may want to add.

It's all about thinking outside the box; using what you have and taking it to a new level to arrive at where you want to go!

Modern Graphic

A fresh, fun, contemporary look that combines urban styling (imagine a downtown loft) with edgy, colorful elements and midcentury design. Simple furniture forms balance out bold accents and patterns. Think the Museum of Modern Art, Frank Lloyd Wright, and a Rubik's Cube.

Features:
Furniture with clean lines and no extra adornment. Blocks of saturated color mix with boxy upholstery with plain legs or skirt less bases.

Lacquered finishes and a mix of woods, both light (birch and oak) and dark (walnut and mahogany) help to create this smooth, clean sophisticated appearance. Geometric or abstract patterns and Pop Art–inspired accessories complete this look.

In each of these design styles we will show two examples of architectural styles and address the challenges of each.

The photo shown in the above example is an obvious fit for this style. Let's try a totally different point of beginning.

This is a very modern apartment but also found in many newer or remodeled homes. It is a simple transformation. All of the walls work just as they are. Light colors that blend into one another allow the eye to travel to the furniture and accessories. It is almost stark but is saved by the simple straight lines of very comfortable contemporary furniture. Pendent and track lighting are perfect for this design.

Furnishings should include clean lines and no extra adornment. Blocks of saturated color mix with boxy upholstery with plain legs or skirt less bases.

Lacquered finishes and a mix of woods, both light (birch and oak) and dark (walnut and mahogany) help to create this smooth, clean sophisticated appearance. Geometric or abstract patterns and Pop Art–inspired accessories complete this look.

If you have furniture that is drastically opposed to this style you can use strictly tailored slipcovers in light or very dark colors. Add geometric or striped pillows on the sofa. Let's assume you really love the accent shown, the animal print ottoman being used for a coffee table.

You can build a cube from inexpensive wood or use a very traditional piece you already own and transform it. Consider lightly roughing up the finish and applying spray on glue (found at most hardware stores) and then apply fabric to the piece. Natural woods work nicely in this design, but if you have battered furniture that you cannot imagine using, either sand lightly and apply spray Minwax in the color you are working with or simply paint the piece in high gloss white or black to compliment this design style. Add poly as a top coat to prevent rings and stains on your newly finished tables.

Contemporary floor lamps and simple clean and sophisticated accessory pieces will make you proud in this room!

Contemporary vinyl blinds are typically found in this design as window coverings. The goal is sleek, modern and sophisticated throughout.

Natural wood floors and tile floors are perfect here. Add oversized thick rugs, even if you have carpet. Try to remain in the black, white and silver color tones for the accessories with a punch of red or contrasting complimentary accessory pieces.

But, if you have the style shown below to work with, we have a little more work to do!

This home is very traditional; ceiling height is 9'.

The floors are beautiful but outside the preferred colors and finishes that compliment this design style. We have plenty of natural lighting with the sliders, a plus.

Paint is our first change in this transformation. Normally I do not recommend high gloss paint. However, in this design it is complimentary. Try using a bright white on all the wood trim in the room in high gloss enamel. Use the same color in flat paint on the ceiling. Continue the same color in eggshell or satin finish on the walls. We need to create a blank canvas that will not direct the eye to any detail of the room design. Smooth and sleek is the goal!

The traditional chandelier must be replaced with a really contemporary design or with modern track lighting. Either will compliment this room.

Using vinyl blinds in this room may be a big mistake, resulting in the look you find in every apartment community.

Let's try vertical wood blinds like the ones below. If this is not in your budget, we will look at a drapery option as well.

These blinds create the correct look and feel in this setting. If you intend to continue with the floor color as shown, match the blinds! We want a smooth transition in the room!

Drapery options that will also work are as shown.

This very simple flowing ringed drape is inexpensive and brings the metals back in. You an create this from sheets and add the rings which you can purchase at any fabric store or even discount stores. If you purchase rings, spray them in high gloss silver spray paint to match your accessories.

This simple rod pocket design will work equally well in your new room. All of the furniture details in the first example apply to this space. We simply had to create the proper setting. Change out the wall plate electrical covers with chrome for added detail.

Cozy Casual

A warm, traditional look made for relaxing with family and friends. This style draws on English and early-American furniture designs, as well as laid-back country, cottage, and farmhouse styles. Weathered, low-maintenance furnishings are easy, inviting, and built for daily life. Think golden retrievers, fuzzy slippers, and just about any movie that reflects a Rockwell Painting theme.

Plush upholstery, often slip covered, with roll or square arms and skirts or ball feet.

Indestructible tables with turned legs, trestles, or substantial pedestal bases define this style. Think warm wood tones with rustic or distressed finishes and natural fabrics, like cotton and wool; these fabrics work beautifully with Cozy Casual design styles.

Solid textiles, simple stripes, or unfussy floral patterns in muted colors complete this look.

Vintage Eclectic

A rich, layered look combining flea-market finds, furniture designs from various time periods (including Victorian pieces and 18th-century French styles), and a diverse collection of accessories and artwork. Dusty colors, timeworn or handmade textiles, and collected objects create a lived-in feel. Think Paris flea markets, Granny's teacups, the film Grey Gardens.

Features: Furniture with shapely, feminine silhouettes, intricate detailing, and weathered finishes are all about Vintage Eclectic.

Jewel tones mixed with washed-out, chalky shades; Antique and vintage elements interspersed with newer, offbeat items.

A varied mix of fabrics (on pillows, upholstery, and window treatments), including jacquards, paisleys, ethnic tapestries, folk motifs, botanicals, and floral designs, Crystal chandeliers and embellished lamps; Abundant art and decorative accents on walls and surfaces.

Older homes lend themselves to the vintage look and feel architecturally as this style is duplicated from their origins.

The photos shown depict homes likely constructed from the 1940's forward. Notice the high ceilings; crown moldings have been replaced with smaller, simpler board and left over's from the Victorian era pop up in the accessories.

Wallpaper is abundant to create this style. Flocked wallpaper particularly lends itself to this design but the beauty of vintage eclectic is the word eclectic. It allows you to use anything you to create a cozy inviting environment with a plan!

This creates an artsy environment that is cozy, comfortable and beautiful.

How can that work in this type of home?

The low ceilings, lack of natural lighting, boxy architectural design, and baseboard heating and worn carpet make this feel impossible.

While wood flooring is more suited to this style, let's assume that you are stuck with this flooring because it is a rental or new flooring is not in the budget.

When you have low ceilings combined with a lack of natural lighting you have to address those issue with the walls and flooring. We have beige carpeting here so the examples being shown reflect this shade. You can do the same when making your choices based on what you currently have if you are going to keep it.

Something light that draws our attention up will make the room feel bigger and the ceilings feel higher. is in order if you are wallpapering this room

Geometric cube design with contrast of whites will create a feeling of texture and depth.

This is called scribble paper, referencing the free flowing design. It feels like it can go on forever, all the way up!

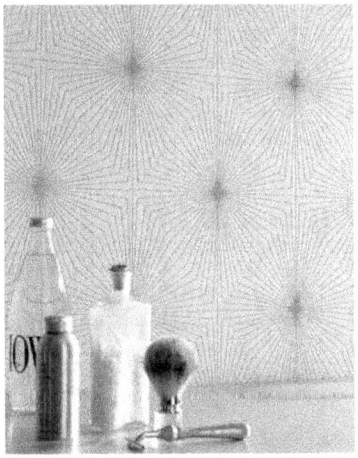

Another geometric pattern that instills a sense of expansion in the room.

Very traditional and pretty! This kind of design is available in almost every complimentary color. Just remember the idea of LIGHT colors to make the space fell lighter and larger.

This paper has replaced the damask from the last one and uses foil and circular patterns extending the eye up, up and up. This paper is a little more modern, yet still very vintage.

This pattern is a little busier bur the vertical lines draw the eye upward; the design is smaller but quietly repeated and will work nicely. The furniture in this photo is a good example of vintage. It has been repainted and looks great! Notice the modern glass mirror coupled with the older pieces. The COLORS of the painted pieces make the statement.

I'm not wallpapering; maybe because it is a rental, maybe because the budget does not work with wallpapering or maybe you simply hate wallpaper or have heard horror stories about removing it. (The newer papers with the correct installation are easily strippable). Let's paint instead!

In this illustration we have low ceilings and a lack of lighting. This commands light paint. You can use nearly any shade in the eclectic theme. Just pick the lighter hues to allow the room to visually 'grow.' Stay with one paint color in the room and avoid accent colors in a darker shade. It will only break the travel of the eye and make it feel smaller.

If possible, convert your baseboards to bright white. A low ceiling demands bright white paint to 'lift' it up.

If you have the cut out area shown in this photo, referred to as a pass through from kitchen to dining rooms, it is time to make it disappear.

Depending on your theme in the room, one of these options may work nicely for you. Beaded curtains come in every color imaginable including metallic if you are interested in a more hip feel in the room!

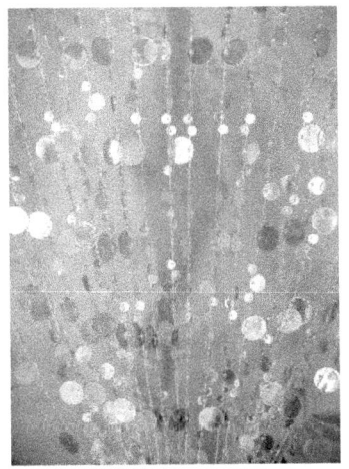

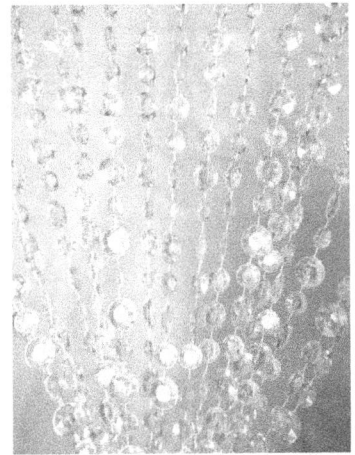

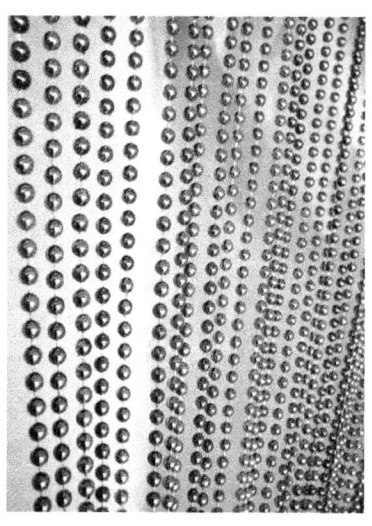

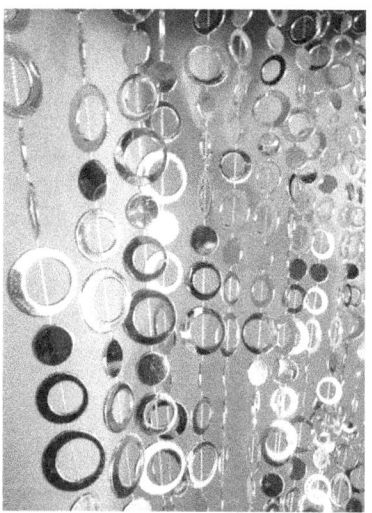

While we were only addressing the opening in this room, these curtains all come in lengths of 84 inches. You can easily cut them to the desired length. Let's leave them all the way to the floor and lose the exposed baseboard for no extra expense.

If you don't have anything you need to 'hide' you can buy the least expensive, which will be the shortest, and then cut them to fit just below the opening or whatever length is desirable to you.

This style loves the old 'early junk' collection of furniture! Yard sales, garage sales, thrift stores, Craig's List and a multitude of other places will provide any accessory you are missing. Mix, mix and mix some more.

If you are stuck with carpeting you hate, clean it and then add rugs you find in thrift stores.

Modern mirrors or ornate older ones work equally well. Paint them in metallic or complimentary colors and just be YOU!

Victorian Styles

Two rooms are pictured in this example. Both are a perfect representation of the luxurious, ornate and comfortable style of the Victorian era.

Interior spaces bathe in nobility and class, showing off expensive fabrics and elaborate pieces of furniture. Here is what designers like to call the most luxurious, gilded design style which surprisingly is, at the same time, cozy and comfortable.

With its name and origins drawn from the Victorian Age (period named after the reign of Queen Victoria), this lavish and sophisticated style develops royal features, residing in the excessive use of furniture, fabrics, patterns, floral motifs and other accessories.

Architectural components such as coving arches, cornicing and ceilings are considered key elements in obtaining the Victorian aspect. You can easily turn your plain room surfaces into Victorian masterpieces with specific decorative details like bas-reliefs with nature motifs, carvings and moldings.

Because Victorian relies on ornate wall coverings, rich, full window treatments and lots of 'stuff' you can pretty much make this style work in any home. If you live in a traditionally designed home you need only choose the perfect paint or wallpaper color to compliment your color scheme and change out the lighting. In this design style, it is all about the accessories, wall hangings, lighting, furniture and drapery, lots of it! This era of furniture and accessories is abundant in thrift stores and on line.

If your home has the typical 4 inch baseboards try adding an additional trim piece. You can buy these, prefinished and very ornate, at Lowes or Home Depot very inexpensively. Pick up the contractor glue while you are there and make this really easy!

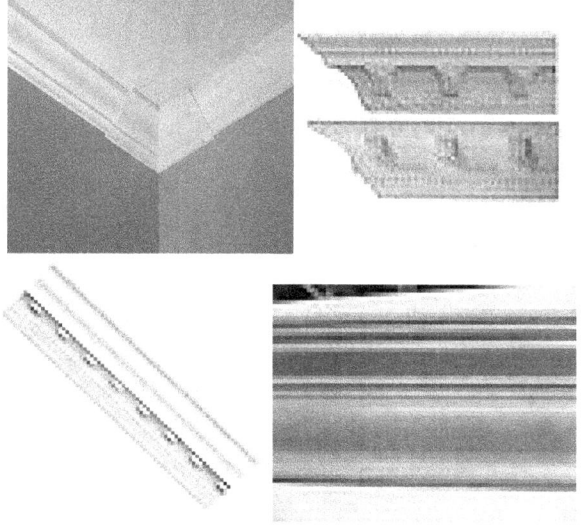

Be creative! If you have furniture that looks nothing at all like this and you are stuck with using it then add complimentary throw pillows that do reflect this era. You can sand the wood pieces lightly and apply dark cherry or mahogany Minwax and create a totally different look to the pieces. No fear!

Look for ornate lighting, candles, trays and massive mirrors and just go with the flow. The window treatments are vital here. Look for deals on velvet or velvet look-alike drapes or satin drapes. If you love your very plain drapes but they won't work pick up complimentary colored tousles at the fabric store and some stitch witchery. You can pick up tasseled trim for the lamp shades and use fabric glue to bring them into this era. In minutes you will have transformed your old contemporary drapes into beautiful Victorian drapes. This same works to create matching pillow for the sofas.

Flocked wallpaper is the best choice for this design plan. The typical colors range from burgundy to a rich cream color and soft white with lots of gold in the accent pieces. Royal blue was frequently used as an accent color in this era.

For accessories, pick up gold or bronze spray paint and re-purpose your lamps, picture shades and mirrors to create the Victorian look.

Wooden floors are the best option to easily transform a traditional space to Victorian. If you don't have them and can't get them, try to locate a room size rug. These are in abundant supply and inexpensive. Try to stay within your color scheme as you search for gold's, burgundies, royal blue and cream colors to set the stage for flooring.

What if this is your room challenge? What could be further from our desired Victorian plan?

This room has 12 foot ceilings and is flanked by wall to wall windows. There is very little opportunity to use baseboards or ceiling trim. We have a really 'high tech' feeling in this room; the Berber carpet is a far cry from our desired plan as well.

Victorian design does not promote light, airy or bright in its best setting. In fact, it is the exact opposite. It is opulent, with heavy window treatments to maintain privacy and a rich ornate feel in the room.

Wallpaper in this room will make a really big difference in how it feels. Take a look at the following samples.

This transformation will likely require all the walls to be wallpapered. The last sample is the most versatile; the first sample that is blue and gold is equally quiet and elegant.

These next pictures reflect the essence of the Victorian era and are a good source of inspiration.

Envision the colors and look and feel before you begin this process

This picture is a reflection of the traditional Victorian Era drapes. Add this to the room we are creating, covering all of those windows and we have an entirely new space. If you simply cannot afford all those drapes, look for the color that suits your that fits you design plan in traditional drapes from a discount store and use the method above, (the tassels and stitch witchery) and make them in only a few minutes. If that is not possible, use the same process with sheets; I suggest white with gold trim. The trim is what makes this statement.

If you have the funds (not a lot) you can buy the plastic insulated trim and apply to the windows to create beautiful paned windows.

This room has commercial grade Berber carpeting. I think you would be well advised to pull it up and simply paint the floor if you are not able to install wood flooring now. Whether your subflooring is concrete or wood, it will paint nicely if you sand off the high spots and apply 2-3 coats and then add a coat of poly to keep the shine. Then add large rungs to complete the cool.

Painted floor with stencils added.

The architecture in this room suggests that you will find canister and track lighting. If you have canister lighting (recessed in the ceiling) you can pick up a tiffany design in Plexiglas and cut to fit the inside of the lights.

Pendant lighting like the one shown below is also available very reasonably.

If you have track lighting in the center of the room where you would typically find a chandelier, replace it with a chandelier.

Then add floor lamps and table lamps where space permits:

Budget permitting you can add prefinished molding to the baseboards to increase the size and also as crown molding. This was detailed in the early part of the Victorian discussion.

The furniture detail is the same as in earlier part of this chapter. Do not be afraid to use spray paint on your accessories, frames and furniture. Metal tones are available very inexpensively. For lamps, paint them and then just change the shade to a one with a Victorian look.

 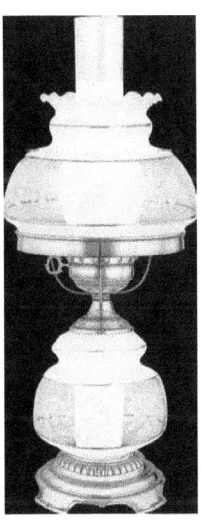

Don't shy away from thrift stores and auctions to find the extra accessories or furnishings you are missing. Auctions are shamefully inexpensive on Victorian furniture and accessories.

Very inexpensive pedestals as shown here are a wonderful way to bring in the charm of the Victorian era without blowing the budget. Pick up two and add a random piece of glass for a great entry or sofa table. Single pedestals hold decorative bust's and look beautiful and very elegant.

A finished spectacular Victorian room!

Tips: Try painting tables in the room gold; then add marbleized spray paint for the top! Make sure you add poly to create the 'marble' shine.

Discarded 6 panel doors are a perfect 'paneled screen'. Collect them at Habitat for Humanity or on Craig's List and paint or stain. Connect with hinges and you now have a wood paneled wall!

Add ceiling medallions to showcase a chandelier or important lighting component. These are available in white, gold, bronze and a multitude of colors. If you want to create something unique and spectacular by using Rub 'n Buff metallic finishes to create your own personalized design. This also gives a metal finish to wood furniture and will enhance all the wood pieces you paint by adding it to the legs and base of the furniture.

Modern Minimalist Style

Modern Minimalist is the complete opposite of Victorian. This style is a form of extreme accuracy; nothing is too much, without heavy backgrounds. The emphasis is on simplicity, the colors may be dull or bright, in any case flashy colors. Pieces are either geometric shapes – square, rectangular, round, but the surfaces are clean, no scenery, no details. Minimalist modern style by its name, illustrates the simplified forms.

Furniture with clean lines and no extra adornment showcase this style. Blocks of saturated color mix with boxy upholstery with plain legs or skirt less bases.

Lacquered finishes and a mix of woods, both light (birch and oak) and dark (walnut and mahogany) help to create this smooth, clean sophisticated appearance. Geometric or abstract patterns and Pop Art–inspired accessories complete this look.

Indestructible tables with turned legs, trestles, or substantial pedestal bases define this style. Think warm wood tones with rustic or distressed finishes and natural fabrics, like cotton and wool; these fabrics work beautifully with Cozy Casual design styles.

Solid textiles, simple stripes, or unfussy floral patterns in muted colors complete this look.

This style is easily created in contemporary architectural designed homes. Simple, straight walls, many free standing (does not reach the ceiling) angled ceilings and even plant shelving works perfectly for this style.

Windows in the contemporary home are typically long and narrow and lend themselves to no curtains. If yours do not, pick up a couple of rolls of tinted window film. This is an inexpensive idea to provide complete privacy, reduce harmful rays from harsh sunlight and create the minimalist look.

Once applied you will have the same effect you see in commercial buildings. You cannot see in from outside; rather it appears as a mirrored image.

Tiled floors are perfect for the minimalist look. If you do not have a solid surface floor I urge you to take a look at the Victorian chapter addressing tearing up the flooring and painting the subflooring. A neutral blue gray with a poly finish is the look you want to achieve. Check the Color Your World chapter for detailed instructions on floor painting.

Your walls should be painted in light blue grays or shades of muted whites. The woodwork should not create a break visually so try using the same color as the walls in a higher gloss.

Rugs are not necessary nor do they lend themselves to this style. Think minimalist!

The furniture is sleek and also minimal. You can repaint or refinish all of your pieces; try using nickel plated spray paint, chrome or high gloss black or white to achieve this look. If your current furniture has decorative trim, remove it before painting. The look will be totally transformed.

The chrome paint is excellent for the legs; switch to a high gloss black or white for the tops of the tables and add sleek hardware to the pieces.

If this room looks more like the one you are attempting to convert; we have a few challenges to overcome!

For this makeover we begin by painting the walls in washable flat paint. Pale blue grays blend well with the nickel and chrome colors that compliment this style. We need to minimize the ornate woodwork so that it visually fades into the walls. Match the color and use satin or eggshell paint (low sheen) on the woodwork. The ceiling should be bright white and reflect the light down. Standard ceiling white will accomplish this.

If your budget will permit sanding and refinishing the floors to a neutral light color will work wonders to diminish the visual changes you experience in this room Modern Asian bamboo influenced stain is perfect.

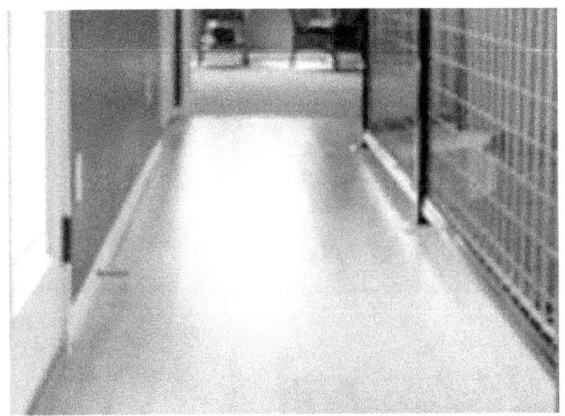

This is light and airy and will blend into the walls. You have an equal stark effect by using a very dark wood stain like espresso. It appears clean and sleek.

Otherwise, white paint will do the job for very little expense

The windows and bay area are a complete deviation from the style we want to create in this room.

Hanging natural rice paper shades in a color that matches the woodwork will promote a sleeker appearance. Pull them down to the floor to create the long narrow look you want for the windows in the room. These shades are very inexpensive and will accomplish the goal. The shades come in a

variety of designs. The simpler look is best for this style.

Look for a piece of furniture that takes advantage of the angles in this room. A half circle piece will totally remove the visual impact of the wall; drawing the eye to the furniture rather than the architecture. The console table pictured is a perfect fit to draw attention away from the bay windows and into the style.

The pieces shown below will accomplish the same goal. Acrylic is also available for less money; however, a clear acrylic will defeat the intention of drawing attention away from the architecture..

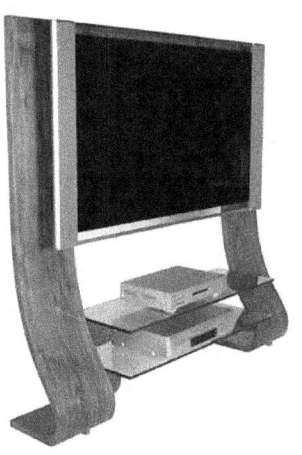

Shopping thrift and garage sales may not be as fruitful for this style as online purchases and Craig's List.

You can use older modern pieces that are readily available at thrift stores and simply paint them to match your color scheme.

Wall hangings like the one pictured blend well with the Modern Minimalist style.

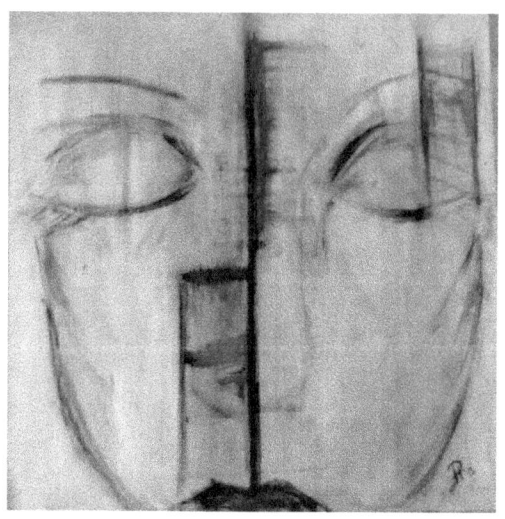

Avoid rugs but add texture with clean lines on the sofa accent pillows and accessories. A room without texture is cold and uninviting.

Rustic Style

Rustic is an interesting style. It conjures up thoughts of mountains and sweeping views and crackling fireplaces.

The style structure is crude, featuring rough, natural details; structure elements of furniture and lighting can be in tree trunks, logs, branches, jute. This style is typically found in mountain vacation homes, and rural areas.

If you love this style and live in a log cabin, you're in luck! This is a made in heaven marriage. The images previewed here reflect the typical design of the rooms.

Open spaces, inviting furniture that begs you to curl up and enjoy the view and the fire work perfect in living areas. Even if your furniture is not made out of rough hewn logs, you can substitute this with older heavy solid wood pieces that are found in nearly every thrift store.

Wall colors should be deep and rich; Pine Yellow, Deep Rich Brown and Hunter Green are complimentary to this design style.

Sherwin Williams offers this guide as their Rustic Refined Collection. It is a good place to begin. You can pick up samples of the paint at

Lowe's for $3.00 and take them home to try in your surroundings. Avoid very dark colors in small spaces!

Let's take a look at a typical home that is not rustic in design and presents more challenges.

Now what! Let's try two options. Wallpaper is a quick fix for the walls

The first example is light, soft and still conveys a 'stone' feel. This next one is obvious. It turns your interior into a log cabin.

Take a close look at this next one. It will transform this very contemporary fireplace area into a rustic dream!

The next few choices are variations that all work to complete this transformation.

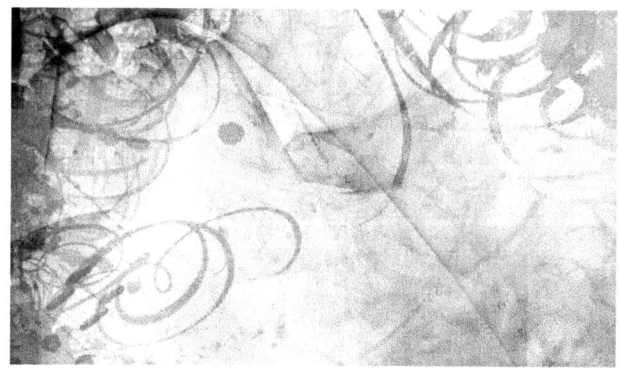

This is a mural that will work in an accent area you want to emphasize.

Limestone brick wallpaper and stone paper is available. You need only decide on your color scheme and then select the pattern that works with it. The ones pictured work well with browns, taupe's, blues and tans.

You can also purchase faux stone and add it to the fireplace area or any area you want to emphasize in this design. Budget permitting you can purchase a rustic mantel or make one. Otherwise, the one shown is a faux mantel and is priced very reasonably.

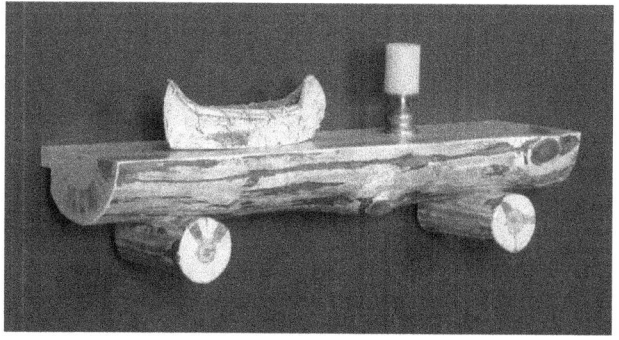

If you opting for paint, this room is darker and will benefit from using lighter shades in washable flat paint. Creamy whites or light taupe would work nicely here.

The ceilings should continue the typical ceiling white unless you have really high ceilings; if so, you can paint them in very light beige.

So, let's imagine the fireplace with the faux stone or wallpaper and the walls in a pattern you have chosen. We have almost created our canvas! But, look at those floors!

If you are renting and stuck with the carpet it is time to clean it and cover it up! Rustic rugs like these are helpful. Finding fake bear skin rugs is perfect! You can make these out of fake fur fabric on a foam backing.

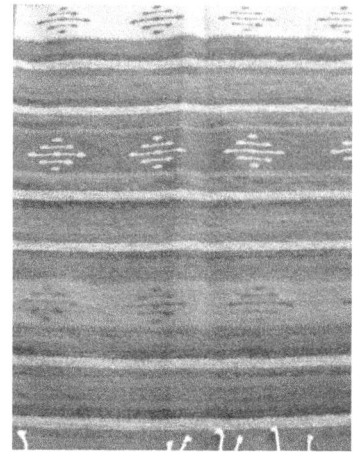

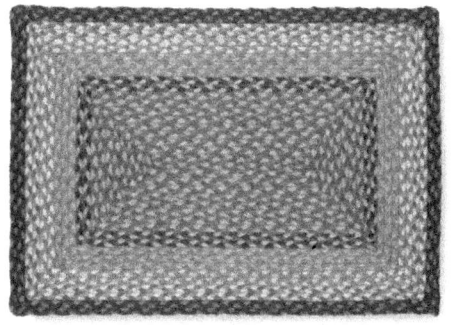

These rugs are readily available so just keep your eyes open in thrift stores, online, on Craig's List, almost everywhere!

If it is possible to change the flooring to wood, that is wonderful. If not, you can pick up half inch plywood and cut the planks in. Then secure it to the sub flooring and stain in a natural wood color.

The sliding glass door is clearly not typical to this style. Wooden shutter doors are available for sliders that actually slide! If you match these to the window shutters you will create a truly rustic ambiance. Then add the rugs.

If that isn't possible, opt for tie-up blinds or the rustic look curtains; draping fabric secured with metal rings will accomplish this look.

If you are even a little handy, you can easily locate actual feed bags from your local tractor supply or online and *make them*!

Look for simple pieces of furniture in your house to repurpose. You can paint the pieces in a natural wood color and reinvent them.

Your accessories can be changed by merely painting frames with the bronze and copper spray paint.

Don't be afraid to try this on lamp shades and lamps as well. It works! If your furniture is not rustic and not new, create this by using the hammer and chain technique to 'rough up the surface.' This is accomplished by actually beating the wood!

Apply Minwax in the desired color and you will have rustic furniture.

Add baskets and natural accessories to soften the tones in the room.

Classic Reinterpreted Style

This is a refined style, elegant, where classic forms details are found in a new approach. The forms preserves the structure of old forms or parts in general updating them sometimes or some elements of a furniture style combined with modern elements, creating that fusion between old and new. Finishing parts are in a new approach-painted

and varnished, with different and innovative colors, surface gold, silver, finished with patina or serigraphic.

This style is actually a new name for Art Deco. You may recognize it better when referred to in that manner. Art Deco was one of the shortest-lived design periods in history.

All about sensational, freewheeling modern living and daring new designs, Deco was hit hard by the looming Second World War. It was time to pack up the Charleston records, put away glamorous accoutrements and face harsh reality.

But the style never seems to go quietly, or for long.

The reason Art Deco furniture is popular again now is easy to figure. "Art Deco embellishes simple forms, exquisite materials and luxurious finishes to create a truly modern expression. We're comfortable with the familiar shapes and proportions of Art Deco. That's why Art Deco resonates and endures. Art Deco complements both modern minimalism and classic traditionalism.

When we think of Classis Reinterpreted home furnishings, we envision voluptuous leather or velvet upholstered club chairs, sleek lacquered cabinetry, gleaming martini sets and mirrored boudoir vanities. Hallmarks include geometric or rounded silhouettes, inlays and veneers, ornamentation such as starbursts and zigzags, and machine age materials such as aluminum, plastic and steel.

If you're a little bit Artsy, traditional and still love elegance this design style will be a perfect fit for you!

This style can be easily created in almost any architectural setting except typically Rustic designs. Traditional or contemporary, it is more about the furnishings and the overall finished appearance.

Take a good look at the next few photos; notice the furniture, accessories and overall look and feel of these rooms.

These pieces of furniture were released in the very late 1960's and 1970's as 'Mediterranean' and 'French Provincial'.

Mediterranean furniture featured very dark wood with ornate trim added for detail. Frequently the sofas and chairs were covered in velvet or 'crushed' velvet.

French Provincial furnishings were typically white or lighter wood tones, many times with gold stenciled trim.

The examples above reflect the same pieces, some with new upholstery and all with painted wood. What an incredible difference. These pieces appear more formal than some that you have seen earlier in this chapter. However, they are durable and really beautiful in their repurposed glory.

They are much prettier today than in their original state. The lighting is spectacular, if a little bit funky.

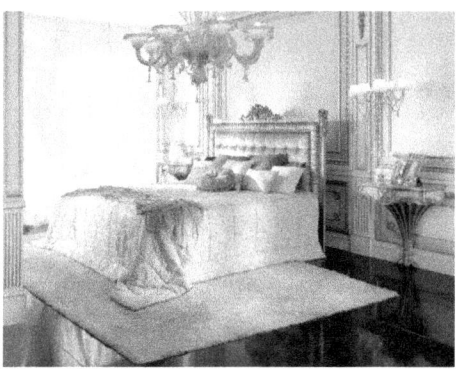

Why all the photos; because, as we discussed in the beginning, almost any architectural design will work nicely for this style. You must decide what pieces of furniture you have to work with and what style you want to repurpose them into; then you can create a design plan with color, flooring and wall choices that go with your furniture plans.

Bear in mind that small spaces are better suited to light walls. But, they can be spectacular walls! By glazing over a standard pearl white paint you have created elegance and interest. You can add pre-finished trim pieces to create detail on the walls if that compliments your plan.

This is your chance to mix some of everything you like and call it a plan. If you do not have furniture pieces that will create the look you envision, decide which pieces you can sell and use the funds to replace the pieces. The pieces you are seeking are vintage; their condition is not important since you are going to be refinishing them to a new look.

Shop thrifty for these pieces; it is not necessary to spend a lot of money. You are looking for solid wood pieces with great lines and detail.

The flooring in your home is not going to be an issue as any type of flooring can work with your plan. If you have wood floors and own the home you may want to consider refinishing them to a darker color or to a silvery white. If not, just select rugs that go with the style you plan to create.

Accessories should contrast or blend in this style. This means painting picture frames or staining them into the opposite side of the color wheel. This is a fun, easy and comfortable selection to work in. Enjoy!

Maverick Style

The Maverick style is a part of the modern style and can even join the high tech style we have discussed.

This approach is very inventive, unusual and unconventional. It is young, explosive, and inventive and does not respect the rules. Structure can be obtained by joining pieces, overlapping volumes and volumes twisting colors can be randomly chosen even for the same room, seemingly nothing happens, only part of the eccentricity of this style.

Eccentric is the operative word here. This style may remind you of your old days at college! The Maverick Style begs for unusual and creative furniture and accessories. You may find that you will blend other styles into this design. For instance, you may love traditional but hate the restraints of that style. Or, love contemporary but don't want the fuss and certainly don't want to look like the rest of the people in your crowd.

In that instance you could easily create your own TV media stand with crates or bricks and a board, paint the bricks into a contemporary color and be at the height of this style.

Notice the enclosed part of the shelving units in the picture above. NOTHING is centered or balanced. This personality begs to be different, ingenious and creative. You can literally make something from nothing and decide which additional style you want to blend in with this one.

You may also be intrigued by cutting edge designs that are simplistic and stark but totally different like the chair pictured here.

When looking for items to add to your collection visit furniture stores that carry commercial (office) furniture. You will find this style is plentiful there. These pieces are on the market for resale frequently and do not command a big price. Look past the manner in which it was intended to be used. You will want to think out of the box with this style. Sleek, clean lines with an unusual twist like an unexpected curve will be very pleasing to you. As you look at your own pieces of furniture and accessories try to visualize the same pieces in a beautiful lemon yellow, lime green or sleek black or white.

Chrome is great but if you don't have it currently, a can of spray paint will make that wish a reality! Even if you are working with a wood surface, go for it.

The Maverick Style discards rules. A loft in Soho is equal to a basement apartment. Cutting edge and unusual is what you are trying to create.

Very simple window coverings or a film covering is your best choice. Even in an older home, consider painting the woodwork in a nice silver tone that makes it appear metal and contemporary.

Expose the windows and make them stand out; you are about being different. Blend the woodwork into the wall color. The typical Maverick Style is created from white on white on white for the ceiling, walls and woodwork. But, anything goes!

For this style you would be very comfortable with tiled floors; or equally so with old wood floors. They simply have to be sleek and unusual and cutting edge to get your attention. If necessary, paint the flooring or remove carpet and paint the floor. High gloss is your goal.

For accessories, check out the 70's era and repurpose the pieces with your new color scheme.

It is not necessary to address how to change an unrealistic room into this style, every design works. This style is about clean concise lines and quirky accessories.

Contemporary Style

The room pictured above is actually a modern contemporary style combo but maintains a contemporary line through selected finishes and the color palette used.

The choices of furnishings are very new, modern, and cool. Colors are balanced, warm, bright tones; pastel can be out of the question when it comes to these styles.

The wood finishes are warm, wood-veneer; solid wood doors with frames that appear to look more polished, and panels upholstered with leather or textile materials may be characteristic of this style. Ideal materials are velvet, plush, upholstered pieces. Jungle print or other animal skins are often used in shaping the ambience characteristic of this style. The chest pictured below is recovered in faux ostrich skin with upholstery tacks added for detail. This was a simple process that involved lightly sanding an older piece with good straight lines, spraying contractors glue onto the wood, and then applying the fabric. The tacks are easily hammered in with a rubber mallet.

Steer away from country styles that exhibit printed plates, vegetable or floral colors and stains. They will fall flat in this design. Opt for solid colors with no fringe or designs on the cushions and throw pillows. This style will not be kind to sofa covers or anything that breaks the eye from a long, sleek line.

Seek out Scandinavian modern style furniture and accessories.

The first photo reflects a traditional 80's or 90's style of architectural design. Notice the light wood flooring, wide slider doors and nine foot ceilings. This is a typical home in the USA. You are seeking colors that define your style. White is a perfect accent on the ceilings, woodwork and trim. Vibrant colors can be used on the walls or on the accent pieces. They can also be used on furniture that you may elect to paint.

Canister or recessed lighting is perfect. In lieu of that, opt for sleek, lightweight pendant lighting, chrome floor lamps that bend and arch and lamps that are simple and sleek in design.

Our lighting section addresses the contemporary and modern styles in detail so you may want to check that out.

White sofas, white rugs and white accessories blend with the deep rich wall colors or accent walls you may want to create in this style.

Chrome and bronze is great, gold is out.

The next picture is a newly constructed home that reflects the contemporary architecture this style is created for. These are very high, vaulted ceilings, tall and wide sweeping windows, recessed lighting and sleek modern furnishings. It is the perfect example of this style.

If you don't have this, build a platform around your bed frame and paint to match your woodwork.

Look for prefabricated nightstands that attach to the wall with no base on the floor. They are inexpensive and really promote this design style. Paint them to match your new platform.

Artwork is specific in this style. Notice the lines and color in this next photo. They are slightly abstract but more free style and modern.

This reflects the style and the colors that blend well with the vibrant accent colors on your walls and throw pillows.

Today's contemporary designs are incorporating darker wood floors with white rugs to complete your new look.

High-tech Style

High-tech style is an innovative modern style, the emphasis being on furniture structure where every detail of combination is not random and it is part of that structure.

Screws, rivets, wheels apparent booms, rough metal finishes, appearances bulbs are specific to this style. The finishes used are often of metal, glass and plastic and wood in small proportions and for parts we find fabric-upholstered as simple as we can, leather. The colors are often dull-gray (brushed nickel), white and small black scale.

High tech is the zenith in contemporary design. It is unusual to simply happen into a home where this is the architectural design unless you have a high rise in a large city. Let's assume you don't and that you need to create it from an average home.

Look closely at the lighting, floors and walls in the first photo. It is high gloss, sleek and very contemporary.

However do we arrive at lighting that will mimic this style? Overhead lighting can be transformed by attaching a strip of sheet metal sprayed with your chrome spray paint. Even a stovepipe will work. This is an extreme canister design. High-tech allows for some leeway in the rough metal finishes.

If you have carpet, tear it out and prepare the floor for painting. You want a high gloss smooth finish. Two coats of poly on the floor will being a very high gloss finish to the floor.

Bar stools and seating can be made from auto wheels stacked up. Even in the bedroom, you can create a chair form them and add an oversized pillow on top.

The furniture should be painted to a high gloss white, black or red, a little like the Asian without any fuss. Eliminating hardware on the drawers if possible is best. You can use wood filler in the existing holes before painting. If you must have hardware look for the most minimal and sleek design possible.

Your flooring and furniture will create the design in this room. However, if the room is not too small you will want to opt for bold paint colors with a contrasting accent wall in this room. If the room is small, select a bright white for the ceiling, walls and trim. Then choose black or red for your furniture color. Think contemporary and minimal when selecting throw pillows and window treatments. Sleek fabrics like satin with no design are good window treatments if you cannot use the window film. You are stripping out the whimsy and replacing it with cutting edge, sleek and high contrast.

Elegant Country Style

This style is at the opposite end of the spectrum of High-tech! It features rural and elegant furniture styles with influences from the English, French or Scandinavian classics. Rural chic is a better description.

Furniture finishes are nice, bright colors; white, pastel colors and forms in this era were taking over traditional furniture, but it does not feature abundant decorations. Surfaces are painted or sometimes have a slight patina.

Many people confuse this with shabby chic. The big difference is the period of the furnishings. Shabby chic loves the very ornate pieces as much as the boxy furnishings.

Loose pillows and a general country atmosphere typically pervade that style.

Not so for the Elegant Country. Scandinavian lines are clean and sleek. They do feature curves and some stark, interesting detail. This design begs for very tailored chair covers, nothing frilly, and tailored simple throw pillows and curtains. Even drapes may be too much unless you opt for very light weight puddled curtains or very sleek white lightweight drapes. Envision country squire; they never want to be perceived as 'country.'

Is fairly simple to recreate this design; look at your furniture. If you have straight lines on the legs you can probably use the pieces. It is easy to change out the color of the furniture by painting or using Min Wax to stain the pieces. If you have wooden floors you are going to want to steer clear of the high gloss maple and oak tones. You want a white bone finish or even a mahogany or espresso finish with white rugs.

Think about adding a piece of inexpensive faux marble to the tops of your furniture in a white or light color with a dark finish on the rest of each piece.

Crystal lamps or accents are very workable in this design. Elegant rather than shabby is your goal in the finished product. If you have the old cherry frames on your pictures, lightly sand the frames and stain them to mahogany or paint them white.

Either dark and rich or white and lustrous is a better choice.

You can use some brass or gold accents lightly in your room. Use Rub 'n Buff on your mirror frames and picture frames for a polished elegant and beautiful finish. It comes in a large variety of colors that you may love. You literally apply this with your finger and rub it in or off. I consider this a staple in redecorating. You can use it on lighting also. It works equally well on wood or metal.

Lighting should be soft and elegant; crystal or a combination of milk glass and crystal will dazzle in this style. Old candlesticks transformed with Rub 'n Buff will be a perfect final touch.

If you have a space that looks like this:

Your challenge is to diminish the very architectural details that typically attract a buyer to this space.

We are looking for soft, elegant and comfortable! Try painting all of the window trim white. Add thick white rugs to the floor and soft sheer white drapes across every window in a clean motion with as few breaks as possible.

The walls should be a pearly white, which is a softer white than this contemporary style typically features. You will need to make covers out of a soft frosted Plexiglas for the inevitable recessed lighting this space features. Then look for crystal chandeliers and wall sconces to soften the stark feeling of the room. Think quality with a soft, quiet elegance throughout the space.

For accessories, a few great pieces are better than a lot of farm house finds. Silver and pewter are excellent accents to this design.

Pick up an electric fireplace in a nice white shade at your Lowes or Home Depot and add for ambiance.

Shabby Chic

Soft floral fabrics and accessories, pale colors, and a mix of old and new define Shabby Chic Style decor.

Shabby Chic Style Furniture features time-worn, romantic styling and solid construction, making them just right for those in search of this casual, comfortable style!

Shabby chic is the dumpster divers dream! You can use almost any style except contemporary or modern and convert to this.

Much like the elegant country style, shabby chic is inspired by the English and French classics. This is a beautiful, cozy, comfortable style but also permits a little more fuss in the finished product. I am going to use several pictures just to illustrate the many ways to create shabby chic. This design almost requires you to paint the furniture. You will need to mix white paint with two thirds glaze and apply several coats. No poly for this style. Instead, you will need a hand sander to bring in the distressed look!

Search for old solid wood 6 panel doors and other stay wood pieces including barn siding.

These pieces are perfect for creating walls that appear to be wood paneled and yet are finished in the distressed look.

Shabby Chic loves crystal! In the lighting and everywhere, it is a romantic, soft look that loves to pretend to be elegant.

This bath is a perfect example of a modern home gone shabby! Bead board mixes with crown molding to shout, "I used to really expensive!"

This is a perfect example of typical shabby chic room. Notice the simple tables that once were described as early American, now in a new kind of heyday as a beautiful shabby chic accessory!

The old armchairs now have brand new white slipcovers with tie downs exposed. Soft floral designs in pink and pastel purples are beautiful accents. It's really all about white and distressed.

You can use marble tops or simple painted wood pieces just be sure to distress the wood! I highly recommend you seek out crystal chandeliers and lamps. You will love the effect of an electric fireplace if you don't currently have one. It is a soft, simple romantic touch.

If you find one that does not have a mantel, add one even if it is an old used one (better!) or a prefabricated one.

Soft light weight window treatments are a perfect match for this style. You can use the old Priscilla ruffled curtains in a sheer white or opt for the very simple sheer white drapes, I have used white sheets many, many times with great results! Shabby wants to be elegant. Add tie backs in ornate gold for a beautiful effect. You're going to love this!

Shabby Seaside

Shabby seaside stays with the distressed look of shabby but the lines are much sleeker. Look for more tailored but decorative throw pillows, lighting that incorporates metals, yet remains delicate and nautical teak wood pieces for accent.

For wall colors think of the colors found by the sea; the sand, the craggy cliffs, the seashells, the skies and the sea.

Metal is used in abundance in the table bases and accessories.

Curtains are typically straight sheer panels hung by metal rings. Curtain rods may be metal and exposed.

Follow most of the shabby chic ideas and incorporate heavier weight fabrics, including canvas.

Accessories like frames and lighting can be altered with the same Rub 'n Buff methods described in the shabby chic; the seaside is a darker finish reminiscent of the lighthouse colors.

Southwestern

Southwestern interior design is characterized as rich texture with earth-tone colors as the main palette; using bright accents of yellow, orange, red clay, and turquoise, hand-crafted objects, and terra cotta or clay tile roofs.

Upholstery is predominantly made of woven fabrics, leather and suede's as well as animal hides. Traditional native clothing and blankets may be used as wall décor.

Wood furniture is popular and may also feature a distressed finish with metal accents. Accents can be anything from hand-painted tiles to painted ceramic pieces with roots in 16th century Mexico.

Native American tribal designs and building elements such as vigas, latillas and built in niches for artwork are also a common design theme in this architectural style. Southwestern style is very "earthy" and organic, and does not translate well to other indigenous areas of the United States.

Almost every architectural design lends itself to the southwestern style.

If you have selected Southwestern as your choice you will surely want to begin with the walls. You can create a leathered look if you want to faux paint but you can also find the same look in inexpensive wallpaper. Earth tones and more earth tones is the name of this game.

If your room is small, lighten up! Use soft creams and pale gold's on the walls and accent with beautiful turquoise lamp shades.

Exposed natural wood is very desirable to this design style. Rough hewn accent pieces blend naturally with polished hand carved figurines.

Adding faux beams to your ceiling (made from foam and inexpensive) will quickly convert your space.

Vibrant colored accessories that conjure up dessert warmth and Native American heritage set a perfect stage for the southwestern design.

Add natural and vibrantly colored pots and woven baskets to create a warm inviting atmosphere.

Wooden floors are perfect and yet, travertine marble tiles work just as well! For floor coverings I like to steer clear of the 'cow print' rungs and opt for really think wool rugs and vibrant multi colored design rugs.

Accessories and lighting that mimic the silver mined in the west are beautiful in this style.

Window treatments are varied. You can use a simple tie up shade or add natural shutter doors to cover your sliders and then match on the windows.

You have some leeway in the throw pillows as well. You can use vibrant emeralds, ruby reds, soft creams with braid in place of tassels and Native American designs.

Take a look at this old and very traditional piece of furniture that was refinished in a crackle finish. This is a good example of how you can reinterpret existing pieces to this style. The top was covered in faux leather fabric.

If you do not currently have a southwestern motif in your furnishings this is a good example of what you can accomplish.

As you look at your furniture remember you can also distress the existing wood tones for this style.

Southwestern is very comfortable with metal accessories and furnishings. You will see metal often used in the legs and even entire tables made from metal with natural colorful tiles for the tops.

You can pick up several different tiles and break them up and create a mosaic table top for under ten dollars. Use your imagination and enjoy your southwestern style.

This is an example of two completely different interpretations of the Southwestern style.

Mid Century Colonial

Colonial decorating was rustic, basic and simple. But the period this decorating style covers lasted for around 300 years – so as time went on, and for richer people, the style became more ornate and lavish.

Ten years ago this was the only Colonial style we talked about. How times change! Today we have Island Colonial (previously known as Caribbean) and *Beach* Colonial! You need a pair of track shoes to keep up these days.

Mid Century Colonial design typically consists of dark wood, simple lines (like Hitchcock chairs) wood and metal headboards and heavy, solid wood tables, dressers and chests.

Fireplaces sported heavy hand carved and very substantial design as shown in the picture above.

Crown molding is a must when you are redecorating into this era. If you do not already have wide baseboards you may want to pick up some prefinished carved pieces and add on to your own existing boards. If wood wainscoting is possible in your budget, add it. If not you can use a wallpaper that mimics the wood look and add a trim board. This should stop at 29" up from the floor.

Wood flooring stays the most true to this design. If you don't have it and you can remove the existing flooring you can easily paint the floor and be right into this design.

Many people have ignored the wood theme and used carpeting, simply adding the rugs that depict this era. Many times a simple room size braided rug will work on a bare painted floor, carpet and actual wood equally well.

Walls can be painted in deep burgundies, ruby reds, hunter greens or the tones of butter cream and white. Avoid the modern interpretations of the colors that appear iridescent or patterned on the wall. A low gloss eggshell, satin or washable flat will work best if you use high gloss enamel on the woodwork.

Shop thrift stores, auctions and Craig's List to pick extra pieces up at great prices.

If you intend to paint the furniture you want to avoid any distressed look and any high gloss paints. This is not a 'shiny' era. Natural dark stains are most desirable. Adding white painted furniture will work well as accents.

Look for high back wing chairs and curved back overstuffed sofas to compliment this design.

This picture is a modern interpretation of the old original colonial style. Small prints on the fabric are typical to this era. Wallpaper is frequently used in Colonial styles; notice how this room, which is in a very contemporary home with 18 foot ceilings, has been transformed by adding the crown molding and a soffit with traditional wallpaper above.

Ornate chandeliers were very popular in this era. Mirrors were created in gilded gold frames or natural wood stained into the dark tones of the era.

Island Colonial

For years we referred to this as the "Hemmingway" style. That morphed into the 'Tommy Bahama Style and Caribbean Style." Today it has become "Island Style.

At the height of her reign (from 1887 to 1901), Queen Victoria ruled over the British Empire which spanned several continents. Because of the infusion of Middle Eastern and Asian cultural influences, Victorian style was extremely eclectic, displaying the elegance, opulence, drama and romance of these other more exotic cultures. By the same token, those British subjects stationed in the British Colonial outposts of the Empire that included Singapore, East Africa, India and the British West Indies, brought with them their language, principles of government, architecture and furniture.

But because they were so far from their beloved Isle, when new furniture was needed, the styles and designs that reminded them of home were adapted to reflect life in the tropics. Furniture in the British colonies of Asia and Africa sported traditional tribal motifs and animal prints like leopard and zebra.

In the British colonies of the West Indies, beds, sideboards, tables and chairs often incorporated local materials including rattan and leather. Motifs, particularly floral ones, and even some of the furniture pieces themselves, took on fanciful aspects and elements. The British Colonial Style that emerged from the habit of British Colonials adapting the comforts of home to their new surroundings is richly traditional, with touches of whimsy and the exotic.

Traditional arrow feet and finials are paired with simulated bamboo posts and cane panels, perfectly illustrating classic British Colonial design.

This design is another that can be created in any architectural design. It works best with darker woodwork and wooden floors. If you don't have that, white will set the same tone in the room.

This style works well with overhead fans that mimic woven fan blades or dark blades with bronze trim. If you have a white overhead fan, use bronze or Spanish bronze Rub 'n Buff for all of the metal parts and paint the blades with a wood tone spray paint like mahogany.

Older pieces blend very nicely in this environment. Look for older tables with metal covers at the base of the legs. You can add odd pieces and blend them by using textured upholstered pieces.

We frequently see the palm tree motif, particularly on the Tommy Bahama brands. You may tire of that after a short time. I suggest you opt for nubby textures in soft island colors for your furnishings.

The walls should reflect the typical whitewash look with a softer cream shade more like the sand. You can add some of your original colonial pieces into this style this evolved from the later mid century colonial style.

Bamboo influenced trim on the sofas and chairs have replaced the fussier look of the original colonial. Things lighten up on the islands!

You are creating a more natural setting with this style; it is relaxed and yet elegant. You can add a mosquito net (about $20.00) above your bed to mimic the 4 poster look. These were necessary on the islands.

Woven shades and shutters are perfect for window treatments. Shutter doors are the best option for sliding doors if you have those to deal with.

Accents in teak wood, distressed bronze mirror frames and dark stain or paint on your picture frames will help you arrive at this style.

You can add animal print chairs or recover the seats and make matching pillows from the same animal print. These animals are native to the British Isles.

Any pieces you can find to add that are constructed in natural wood, bamboo and slate are a wonderful addition.

Use candles freely as they finish this style in a laid back, casual and elegant manner.

Brass and bronze can be mixed with a few crystal accents just to give added punch.

Metal is also freely used in the Island Colonial design in lighting and furniture.

Think white wool room size rugs compliment this style, but so do natural woven rugs will very little nap.

Think cozy, elegant, romantic and casual at the same time and you will have created the Island Colonial.

The dining room below is created from a round pedestal table that was purchased for $10.00, three Chippendale chairs that Goodwill offered for $10.00 for the three of them, a bench that was out for disposal, a hutch handcrafted in 1910 that was set out for disposal and a little bit of ingenuity to arrive at the Island Colonial style.

The seats were recovered to reflect this style; two leftover king sized pillows were covered in a 15 minute task of simply measuring the pillows, cutting the fabric and ironing on stitch witchery to create the seams. The ties were made in the same manner and tacked on. As you can see, fabrics and accessories tell the tale in this style.

Beach Colonial

The very subtle difference between the Island Colonial and the Beach Colonial are reflected in the billowing curtains, bright white of the walls and accessories and a deviation from the heavier furniture to the almost 'beach like' chaise lounge style chairs. Lighting is now very lightweight pieces in place of the heavy wrought iron; taller, narrower and a little more modern.

In an almost seaside variation, the old crown molding has been exchanged for weathered bead board extending 18" down from the ceiling with a trim board. You can do this if you have high ceilings. If you don't, you may want to try bead board on a single wall.

Chandeliers have actually gravitated to crystal in the beach design plan. Choose the burnished or antique gold bases with a lot of teardrops. Wall scones mimic this same look and make the room feel romantic and airy. If you find pre owned lighting and love it, don't forget the Rub 'n Buff technique to make it yours exclusively! The tiniest bit of this product goes further than you can imagine!

This next photo depicts a dining room using the newer colonial lines with a washed out look to the chairs, better known as slightly 'distressed.'

Beach Island style consists of dark woods, light woods and natural woods blended together in harmony, much like 'beach finds'. Create an overall light and airy feel with bright white walls, light weight fabrics and smooth, clean lines.

Old candlestick sconces blend with new accessories. This style is much freer in the flow of the design. Use your existing pieces and paint some if you like, but refrain from matching the chairs to the tables or anything else.

If using baskets in this design plan pick lighter colors, reflecting a sun bleached feeling.

Where can this be created comfortably? Everywhere; it lends itself to nearly any archeticutral design style. This design style is about a light filled room, lightweight fabrics that promote that feeling, a collection of sximple furniture pieces tastefully joined together to create a casual and inviting atmosphere. Stay with the light colors and imagine walking on the beach; then create it.

Chapter 10
Sizing It Up

Before we address the coversion of your furniture to fit your new dream plan, it seems fitting that we should also talk about the size of your room and what choices will work best to help you create your plan.

Tips for Tiny Places:

Small spaces offer a range of challenges and come in a variety of shapes.

From the graduate exchanging home for a dorm room (and usually sharing it) to studio and efficiency apartment dwellers, cottage or bungalow inhabitants, growing families who are searching for a method to accommodate the changing needs of their family, anyone attempting to find a space for their home office and anyone who lives in a city where space is at a premium with a price tag to match; all of you share this challenge.

A castle does not have to have palatial space to feel like a palace.

Dorm Rooms present a special set of issues. You have one room the size of a typical bedroom that must become the 'home space' for two people, include a place to quietly study, relax, enjoy some privacy and provide enough storage for all the 'stuff' young people deem as vital to their happiness. (This includes clothes, shoes, computers, TV's and everything that applies.)

While many dorm rooms come equipped with some basic furniture they rarely work towards creating a home away from home as they imply.

If you are lucky enough to have a good relationship with your room mate, things can get a lot better very affordably.

Shop thrift stores, Craig's List (Under the 'For Sale' section of Craig's List you will find a Free section. This has postings for 'curb alerts' and will allow you to relieve someone of their goods for the price of your gas to pick it up, and that's all) and any other options you can locate. This is a temporary living arrangement; keep your cash for the lean times and get creative!

Put out a BOLO (Be on the lookout for) space saving twin pedestal beds. They take up the same space as the cot you are provided with and offer 6 wide drawers below the bed for expanded storage.

Even if the beds have to be pushed against the wall, you can use the unavailable side for seasonal storage and the important 'stuff' you acquire.

Look for inexpensive open, short shelving units and place them on the closet floor. These will keep spare books, sweaters and jeans easily accessible and leaves the top rod for hanging clothes. Install inexpensive hanging shoe organizers on the interior of the doors.

Search for used night stands that have three drawers. This is not the time or space for the open look. If you do this you will eliminate the need for dressers and open space for one important piece. A desk armoire provides much needed desk space, built in lighting to study, a place for all of your computer and class book storage and, the all important and must have TV. You can close the door and your room is neat; your area privacy is protected when you've finished your work.

Check out the rules on painting your room. If it is permissible, do it! Take a long look at your windows. Adding soft long drapes adds privacy, texture and creates a cozy feeling. They also keep out unwanted natural light when you plan to sleep in! Find complimentary bedding and throw pillows and thick cushy rugs to complete your theme.

Add neutral lamps to the nightstands or opt for wall sconces by the beds to allow each of you the opportunity to sleep without unwanted lights interfering and your tiny, cramped dorm room will become a true haven away from home.

If you have a roommate who is agreeable you will have fun locating these pieces and redecorating. Even the reluctant roommate may have a different attitude when they see your results!

Studio Apartments consist of one room that accommodates the living and sleeping areas and if you are lucky, a full or partial wall separating the kitchen; and one bath.

Take a moment to review the Dorm Room suggestions to make the most of acquiring storage in your apartment.

You may find a 'Murphy bed' (a fold out bed that appears as a narrow wall unit when closed) is built into the space. If so, it's a great way to get rid of the sleeping area when you're not using it.

If not, you can use the same shopping methods described above to find a used one if you cannot afford a new one.

In lieu of the Murphy bed, a futon is inexpensive, serves as a sofa and folds out to a bed for sleeping. All of these are good space saving options to consider.

Smaller apartment size tables for your living room will allow you to create a spacious feeling in your home. Look for end tables that can double as night stands with three drawers if possible. These will provide storage for clothing and lingerie while serving as end tables during the daytime.

Large, thick wool rugs create a sumptuous and homey feeling in the room and add texture. Look for light, neutral colors to increase the feeling of space. This also adds a visual break point separating your living area from your dining area.

The dining area is probably small, but looking for a way to separate it from your living area will make you feel like it's a special area and not an intrusion into the living space.

Look for a small buffet or entry table to place against the end wall. This adds storage for dining linens and anything else you may need. Again, look for drawers! More is better.

Hang a mirror, a special picture or something simple and large above the buffet. Mirrors make the space feel larger.

Once you determine your personal style, look for a 36" table with chairs that slide under the table. This frees up walking space when you are not dining. If you have space for a small tree beside the buffet you will find that it provides a complete separation of the area visually.

Lastly, go to Habitat for Humanity thrift store, consignment stores or any other option where you can locate a gorgeous light to hang above your table. Nothing says an area is special quite so much as the light you grace that space with.

Top your table with a simple and special centerpiece and your eating area is now a dining area that you will love to entertain in.

The kitchen is usually a galley style that has limited floor space. If a microwave is not included in your apartment look for a small one and hang it under a cabinet. Counter space is critical in galley kitchens.

If you have any available space, look for a rolling cart that doubles as a chopping block/prep area and has storage below. You can move it when you're using it and store it out of the way when you're not preparing or cooking food. Use substantial size baskets on the shelf below to store vegetables and fruits.

The keep it simple method will make you feel much less cramped in smaller kitchens. Orderly cabinets increase storage space; clean countertops allow you to use the limited space for food preparation.

Your bath area is likely to be compact. If so, look around. Is there an area to hang a decorative cabinet and increase storage? If so, find one! The biggest challenge in a studio apartment is find a place for the things you require to be comfortable.

If you have a Burlington Coat Factory or Tuesday Morning store near you, they are worth checking out for shower curtains and inexpensive and attractive storage solutions.

A cloth shower curtain will create a warm and cozy feeling even in a small bath area. Thick towels on the towel bars say 'this is my home.' Some things are worth splurging on and I firmly believe these two items are on the top of the list.

Explore the window coverings and paint options described in the Dorm Room section and apply it to your studio apartment if possible.

Efficiency Apartments typically offer a combined living and dining area, a kitchen, separate bedroom and a bath.

Take a moment to review the suggestions in the Dorm Rooms and Studio Apartment sections as they all apply except the sleeping area. You are fortunate to have a completely separate bedroom.

Your bedroom should feel special. You are sharing living and dining spaces; take the time to look for possibilities in your bedroom.

I love to use chandeliers with dimmer switches in bedrooms. You can find really beautiful small chandeliers inexpensively if you shop with the methods we have been discussing in the previous sections.

If that idea does not interest you, look for a really attractive ceiling fan and use the bedside lamps for lighting.

Limit your bed size to a queen unless you have a really large space. Using apartment size furnishings or scaling down the number of pieces in the room will make a dramatic difference in how your room feels.

Paint if possible and visit Chapter 4 'Color Your World' to find the color and shade that provides the look and feel you want in your private space. Add texture with rugs, window coverings (hang from the top of the wall rather than the top of the window to make the space feel much larger) throw pillows and plants and top it off with bedding that compliments your other selections.

Take a good look at the living room space and the bedroom space and see which best supports a small computer armoire to create your home office.

Your living area will benefit from a TV that hangs on the wall or a narrow media cabinet that increases storage if you do not add the computer armoire.

You may want to explore adding an apartment size sectional sofa. These can create a break from the dining room and living room and still provide an open and spacious feeling while adding seating.

Cottages and Bungalows are actually smaller versions of a typical home. Space planning is more important than ever to achieve a homey, un-cramped feeling.

Eliminate clutter wherever you are able to; clutter is the chief offender of small spaces.

Cottages or Bungalows

Simple, smooth lines will benefit the feeling of spaciousness in your cottage. Sometimes the mere thought of a 'cottage or bungalow' conjures a vision of a Victorian space complete with curly cues on the lamps and curtains replacing cabinet doors. Lose that image!

Cottages benefit from the Seaside and Country Cottage designs that combine soft colors, upholstered furnishings with clean lines and double duty tables in the living room and dining areas.

All of the ideas presented in the 'Dorm Room' sections apply in small spaces. Visit the

Efficiency Apartments section to enhance those ides to cover dining and kitchen solutions.

Most of all enjoy the homey and comfortable atmosphere that is gained from a small space! It makes a large statement if you capture the charm and make it yours.

As you are creating your new space, keep these tips in mind. Cramped spaces become creative places and stuffed rooms become stupendous!

Smaller spaces require less of evrything to make a grand statement. Your final goal in the smaller space is to create a feeling of open, airy and inviting. This means lighter colors, bright white ceilings, no dark accent walls, light floring; nothing should break the visual impact except our furniture and the accessories.

Hide woodwork from windows and doorways by using the same color of the light walls in a higher gloss paint. Keep in mind that flat paint hides defects in the walls. High sheen reflects every ding.

If you have a finish on your walls that does not work with your plan, for instance, your plan is for high tech room and your walls are finished in a texture design, opt for the flat paint. You want to literally create a clean canvas and then paint your picture with the furnishings and accessories.

If you have the opposite challenge, you live in a home with a wide open floor plan and your plan requires a cozier atmosphere the following tips will help you arrive at the desired look and feel.

Escaping Open Spaces:

In the last twenty years a 'new' concept of homes became popular. Gone were the square parlors, traditional living rooms, separate dining rooms, isolated kitchens, enclosed family rooms and square bedrooms with small closets! It's all about open spaces now as that trend has continued. The good news for those who like a lille more cozy atmosphere is that this decade the builders have realized too much is tough to sell.

Open spaces deliver challenges and opportunities simultaneously. Here you are, moved into this new and better home that is open from the front door to the kitchen! What to do?

On the up side, you can choose your dining area. Get creative and see what area feels like a relaxing space; one that has the best view and some access to the delivery of the food will create an easy flow and feel natural.

This floor plan typically defines the builder's idea of the dining area by the placement of the chandelier. That's not a game changer for the 'How To Turn Mundae Into Magnificent' warrior.

Lighting is easily changed from room to room if you love the one you're with and with a replacement if you don't.

A note of caution; before you rush out to buy lighting, decide what style, yes style, is your style.

Take a long look at your furniture, your paint selections, your accessories and the look and feel you want to create in each room.

Lighting is one of the most strategic tools in the game plan of creating your masterpiece. Use it wisely to define an entry area, a dining area and any other 'specific' areas in this floor plan.

In this kind of floor plan, living rooms usually need to be created by furniture selections and placement.

Open floor plans are devoid of wall outlets except against the walls which, as you may have noticed, are missing. Attempting to use table lamps will leave you with exposed cords that impede traffic flow and create unnecessary fall risks.

These floor plans work better with floor lighting and wall sconces that promotes a more comfortable and cozy atmosphere.

Storage is another challenge in the open floor plan. Decide whether you want to create an entry area or foyer and work from that point of beginning.

Placing an entry chest or buffet style of furniture at the point where you want to 'end' the entry area will provide a place for paper and pens to jot down notes or messages at the door and a place for sweaters and other light wraps you grab on the way in or out of your home.

Open shelving units will maintain the open feeling, create a break point and still provide some light storage if drawer units are located in the bottom sections. We'll be looking at furnishings and where to find the things that best suit your design ideas later in this book.

This same challenge is encountered in the family room area and can be addressed in the same manner. The best part of an open floor plan is the walls you do not have to relocate!

The open floor plan usually offers "plant shelving" to accommodate floating walls. These become a display area for your most valued treasures that are stored in many attics for lack of a place to show them off safely.

And one more thing; if you have vaulted ceilings you now have very tall walls. Make good use of them! Look for shelving or older free standing cabinetry units, repurpose them and 'hang 'em high!'

This is a wonderful place to showcase something important in your décor plan.

You can find every style of pre-built fireplaces at your local Lowe's and many other places (back to the online search here) and create your best focal point by placing it under a hanging unit.

You also acquire that much talked about mantle for hanging stockings and a romantic setting for the cozy evenings with this kind of unit. They also have a heater and blower hidden behind the glowing 'fire, making them a very practical solution to a cold room!'

It's a given that having an unlimited budget leaves every door open in your selection. If not, take heart; we have a plan!

We will be devoting a few chapters to furniture placement and how to create specific and defined areas in your home. Those chapters may be very beneficial to you.

Chapter 11
Barely Get Along Street Rocks!

Before we get to the exciting stuff, like transforming your furniture, I would like to tell you a story that may be of assistance as you choose your pieces to work with.

Once upon a time, in a very prosperous kingdom, a district was referred to as 'Barely Get Along Street;' the area was filled with homeless, hapless individuals who had not yet learned to be prosperous.

Others in the Kingdom frequently 'threw them a dime' and donated their cast offs to this area. And, so it was that no one wanted to be associated with 'Barely Get Along Street.'

That was then, this is now! The 'Barely Get Along Street' district has become hip and chic. It *rocks!*

The residents in the kingdom wasted many opportunities and fell into the trap of complacency and soon their prosperity was siphoned off, knights lost their commission in the royal palace and a pall fell across the entire kingdom.

Although everyone was affected, the people who knew best how to navigate this state of affairs all seemed familiar with the 'Barely Get Along Street' District.

As they watched their comings and goings much was written about the people in this area. The perception that they had no choice was quickly replaced by the knowledge that they had made a better choice!

These residents found great value in the 'stuff' other people tossed without a thought.

They looked harshly at waste and pollution of the kingdom and beyond, and worse still, their homes were just as nice as the highest family in the royal hierarchy.

They dressed nicely and had little or no debt for the collector to come knocking at their door demanding their hard earned dollars.

All across the kingdom residents began to watch how these people operated in their daily lives; it was the dawn of a new era!

One where we are all responsible for our actions and where hands that reached out were touched in a beautiful way by people who had never before reached out!

Dumpster divers posted their wares at a place called Craig's List; and their goods were very valuable and affordable!

No longer were there cast offs with a long life time yet to be lived stacked into a disposal pile. Someone fell in love, again, and the cycle of recycle became the norm.

Thrift stores popped up at every corner of the kingdom, even near the palace. Owners whose efforts were not successful in selling their goods consigned them to a better salesperson.

At every turn in the kingdom the residents were treated with the opportunity to find better quality items at more affordable prices and; to make them theirs! How you may ask?

By repurposing! Everyone's doing it now. We have discarded the idea that new cheap particle board furniture is preferable over used furniture!

The savvy buyer today looks for great quality, sturdy wood and a look and feel they can relate to.

They take it home and change it to fit their own dream home plans and the cycle continues.

Debts were cleared from the books in the kingdom; families began sharing time together repurposing their new finds and laughter once again permeated the kingdom!

This resulted from the diminished stress the residents of the kingdom were feeling, having tossed the notion that they had to 'be' anything accept what they were comfortable being. And life was good again!

The most recognized shopping spots in today's 'Barely Get Along Street' districts are eBay, Goodwill, Salvation Army and Craig's List.

These are quickly joined by Habitat for Humanity Thrift Stores, other thrift stores, consignment stores, yard and garage sales and classifieds in your local newspaper.

Once you see what terrific finds are available you will be inspired to join as a seller to repurpose your pieces that no longer fit.

Ah! There is joy in the kingdom!

A word of caution:

Do not make buying trips to a strangers home or invite strangers to your home for selling items alone.

Ask a friend or neighbor to join you. There is safety in numbers! If you feel anything odd about the transaction use your shoes to win the battle and walk away. 'Gut instinct' has saved many a person from a bad experience!

NEVER send payments by Western Union or any other method to a person you cannot meet or to a place you cannot get to or in.

Discard any ad or response that relates a sad sack story about the person having to leave the country but keys etc. will be mailed to you. They won't.

I avoid any Craig's List ad that does not include a telephone number. I rarely respond to emails. Let them call you. You can make a better judgment on who you are dealing with if you hear their voice and the sincerity as they talk with you.

Don't accept checks or money orders for payments. My youngest son has just given his second vehicle away, complete with title to a stranger who first gave a Postal Money Order and the last time produced a Cashier's Check.

Both were worthless paper. Both are hopeless situations for him. These crimes are rarely solved.

If your buyer is not comfortable bringing all the cash, accept a deposit and let them bring it back when they pick up the item.

Don't set yourself up for a failure, or for unnecessary danger.

If your budget is nearing the bottom of the barrel keep a vigilant watch on the For Sale 'Free' section of Craig's List. Many people discard really good pieces by posting a 'Curb Alert".

These people do not have the time or the inclinations to attempt a sale but are happy to see someone who can use their things take them away. Imagine!

Personally I have never heard of a bad experience with curb alerts. The price tag alone (FREE) suggests this is a good deal!

When you visit a consignment store, don't hesitate to make an offer; this is especially true if you are making multiple purchases.

Consignment prices should always present a value hoped to attain.

Keep it going! Join the sellers queue and collect the value from your items to add to your decorating budget; or donate the items to worthy resellers.

It's a little like early American barn raisings, where neighbors help neighbors and everyone is a pioneer! Skid Row morphed into Skid Rose (as in rose from the ashes!) And all was well again!

And so you see, "Once Upon A Time" has become "Once Upon YOUR Choice!"

Chapter 12
A Diva Diver's Treasure Hunt

After a host of ideas, instructions and directions, it's time to don your magician's hat and pick up the wand!

If you have decided you simply do not have the furniture pieces that you are comfortable with recreating and don't have funds to purchase the right pieces, decide whether you are willing to sell them to raise the capitol to purchase the right pieces. If so, the last chapter has a wealth of information on how to accomplish that goal.

Refinishing furniture is an old art and not at all intimidating or cutting edge. Detailed instructions on how to achieve the 'finish' you want are available online by a simple search.

A Diva Diver's Treasure Hunt is more about how to take the pieces you have to work with and recreate them into the 'style design' you have chosen. It is a bigger challenge and a lot more fun. In fact, it is downright exciting when you see the results!

Take a good look again at your design style and note what things most appeal to you about that style. This is important in the recreation process. Was it the colors, the smooth or ornate feeling, the overall ambience… this is a personal choice but the 'whys' matter.

For instance, the following two photos reflect a very traditional 1970's hutch that the owner had; however, they converted to a southwestern design style and opted to use the bottom of the hutch as a sideboard in their new plan.

This piece becomes...

This piece!

This was accomplished by using liquid sand, lightly sanding the wood afterwards, applying two coats of white primer, applying a coat of crackle in medium blend and adding your color choice. The paint on these pieces was sprayed on for a sleeker finish. A final light coat of antiquing glaze was applied to bring out the crackle and wood grain.

New hardware more suited to the southwestern theme was installed.

Fill in the previously drilled hardware holes with wood filler before you begin if you plan on changing hardware.

This piece was finished off by applying the crackle coat to the top and then covering with a piece of black faux leather. The crackle coat gave the fabric a look of natural grain leather.

This transformation allowed the owner to use a very well constructed piece they already had in a new design style for very little expense.

This is another transformation using a faux marble top and ruby red paint.

The next example was presented earlier in the book.

I found this table on the side of the road, hence the Diva Divers treasure hunt theme. The finish was worn and it was on its way to the county refuse site.

But, a closer look revealed that it had great 'bones,' it was sturdy, solid wood and held great promise.

This table required very little sanding the finish was already pretty much worn off. A single primer coat and three coats of deep ruby red paint was applied with a brush and topped off with antique glazing, applied lightly and then wiped off. The hardware was changed to reflect the owners new design plan for the room and this little treasure rose, quite literally, from the ashes to become a beautiful accent piece in the room.

The next photo reflects very traditional end tables from the 1980 that were converted to a Seaside Cottage look and used as a nightstand.

Light sanding and three coats of bright white paint with a clear coat overlay completed this transformation.

The next images reflect an owner who had very traditional furniture and converted to an Eclectic look. This piece was very sturdy and well worth saving; however, the sliding glass doors that were on the front and the boxy free standing bookcase in natural oak was no longer useable to this plan.

The owner committed a lot of time and effort to refinish this into an armoire for her bedroom. The top is covered in 6 inch lace creating an old, antique design. This was covered in poly.

The same lace was applied to the top of each drawer after the initial painting of the piece.

The square design is obviously created by using painters tape. The rest of this design is free hand, finished in a gold high gloss. This is perfect for the artsy look the owner was trying to achieve.

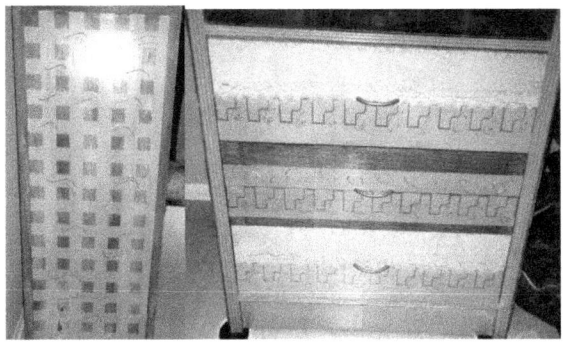

Old Duncan Phyfe tables have lost a little of their luster on the decorating scene. This is typical and it will make a return, but for now, they are easy to come by and coast very little considering the quality of construction. The one pictured below has literally lost its luster!

The owner of this table wanted a distressed look that matched her new décor. She chose the

Country Cozy design and easily created this new look!

This table is another find as a 'Curb Alert' on Craig's List. The price? Free for pickup.

This was achieved by using a base coat with a golden base, topping off with a teal color and sanding the corners and legs lightly to arrive at the desired distressed look.

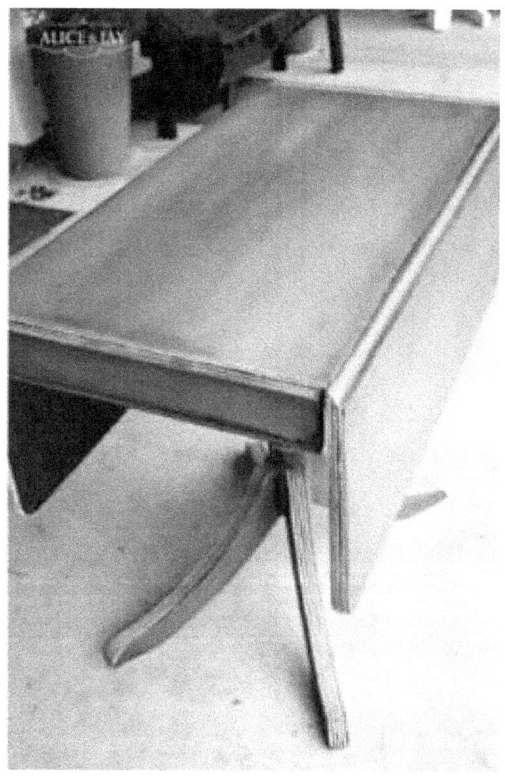

A coat of walnut stain was lightly brushed on to accent the wood grain and then wiped off. A final coat of poly completed this new look.

The distressed look is shown close up in the next photograph.

You can see the first and second coats on this piece, contrasting colors. Yellow gold was used to add an old world richer base to the furniture.

To create a sideboard for the room the owner located an old French Provincial dresser at a Kiwanis store for $50.00 and painted only the highlighted sections you see in the next photo.

This very old piece was painted and distress but the owner opted to keep the old drawer pulls and used the cream Rub 'n Buff to finish the metal trim.

This old Mediterranean sideboard was a discarded free piece. It has been repurposed into a beautiful credenza for a home office.

Liquid sandpaper was applied, and then the piece was lightly sanded and painted in a latte shade.

Walnut stain brushed on as a finish coat with a wipe off of the excess finished the credenza. Notice that this owner retained the original ornate hardware.

An old discarded table and a $50.00 dresser transformed this room. There is almost noting you cannot do to achieve the look and feel you need in your space from the pieces you have at hand or are able to locate by searching for free pickup, disposal at the road and thrift stores and auctions.

This was an old, old mahogany dresser that had long since seen better days.

The owner lightly sanded the piece and filled in the holes left from previous hardware. Then very inexpensive fence paint was applied in three coats.

The top was touched up with Mahogany Min Wax.

Newer hardware was added in a mixture of brushed nickel and crystal for a beautiful look.

The next example is a reverse to the ones we've look at. The owner found an old hutch at the auction that had been previously painted and distressed.

The owner used liquid sand to loosen all the old paint and then sanded with a hand sander. The Early American Min Wax stain was sprayed on and wiped off and the piece is totally restored to its former glory.

Another example of a restoration; this table
was returned to its previous glory.

What about those inexpensive tables you pick
up in boxes. Like these…

These are perfect blank canvases to work from. They do not require drawer pulls; this means they can work with modern, contemporary or even high tech if the finish is in high gloss silver or black paint. You can also get creative as shown below.

This next set of pictures reflects a beat up old table, secured at an auction and refinished into a beautiful dining room.

The owner was working with a Mid Century Colonial design plan.

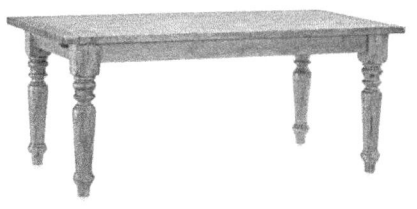

You have been reading a lot about the 'Rub 'n Buff' product in this book. Any stain that you are comfortable with is fine. This product is just overly simple to use.

Although it is advertised for metals and is a great fix for that, take a look at the effect on an old cheap wooden chest.

This requires no sanding, no painting, just a simple application process with appliqués applied.

Min Wax is another product that has been highly recommended. I always keep it on hand. Take a look at simple fixes with this product:

You can use to simply bring back the former richness of the original stain.

What about the overall room change? Let's take a look!

How in the world did this…

Become this?

Simple! The wallpaper was removed, the mantle was taken off, and the fireplace surround brick was removed and replaced with a very simple wooden handmade trim. The floors were painted in an espresso finish and a contemporary room size run added.

This owner opted to sell the existing pieces of furniture and used the proceeds to pick up inexpensive contemporary pieces.

Let's look at an inexpensive kitchen redo.

Before, the room was very traditional and tired. A simple coat of paint on the cabinetry and the addition of a new chandelier in place of the ceiling light fixture produced this result!

Think outside the box!

We can't end this chapter without looking at a bath that has been transformed! Plumbing and electrical was not changed; but look at it now!

This is dark, dingy and totally uninviting. In the makeover, a tub insert with 'prefinished tile look' replaced the shower, the woodwork and vanity was painted and the old commode was replaced. Can you even imagine?

Chapter 13
The Heart of Your Home!

"Creation is always happening. Every time an individual has a thought, or a prolonged chronic way of thinking, they're in the creation process. Something is going to manifest out of those thoughts."

~ Michael Beckwith

The kitchen is the most complained about room in every home seeking a makeover with tenants and homeowners alike. The kitchen is the most used room in the house and wear and tear is evident on cabinetry, countertops, walls and floors.

It also appears as the most substantial room in the house; it is designed to do so. Other rooms have walls, windows, a floor and perhaps a door.

Your kitchen comes equipped with walls covered in cabinetry, appliances and a design you did not choose unless you designed the home or remodeled it to your taste.

Let's assume you didn't. Remodeling your kitchen is an expensive proposition.

Homeowners dream about it and plan for it; tenants attempt to shrug it off, believing there is nothing they can do about it.

Worse, many people assume their own style in a home is defined by the cabinetry.

If you are a homeowner review these potential solutions for Cabinetry:

Painted cabinets in a south Florida home

A

38 year old manufactured home with painted
original cabinetry

Before and after photos of painted cabinetry
(Slightly different angle)

a) The most obvious fix is painting the cabinets. If this is the choice you are making you may be surprised at the myriad of paint treatments available. Study them carefully and choose one that fits your new design plan. These pictures represent a before and after preview of a kitchen. The angles are different but you can easily see they are the same kitchen.

This couple opted for changing out the hardware and adding updated appliances; their completed design plan appeared to be a brand new kitchen. The savings on this room alone was $29,000.00.

b) To get a good finish that you will be proud of, plan on removing all the cabinet doors and hardware.

c) The hardware can be sprayed in a color or finish that compliments your cabinet paint selection.

d) If your cabinets are wood you can rent a small hand sander and rough up the existing finish and smooth out any blemishes.

e) If your cabinets are plastic coated (this is another shocker, a lot of the newer cabinets are coated with plastic to appear wood) look for the application that will adhere to the smooth finish allowing your paint to adhere to the current finish.

f) Primitive and Country designs look great with the bases painted a dark or neutral color; then add barn siding with adhesive and change out the hardware to match.

g) Cottage designs work perfectly with the bases painted white and bead board adhered to the doors.

h) Southwestern designs look great with the spray on treatment that looks like sandstone. Just apply and then spray the poly as a top coat.

i) Budget permitting, you can purchase new doors and finish them with a stain or Min Wax. You will need to sand the bases and apply the same stain treatment or purchase the covers for the bases when you buy the doors.

This process will produce an entirely new kitchen when it is completed.

If you are ready to tear out walls and redesign the kitchen; that's another book.

If you have the space, look for a table with drawers, a buffet that is substantial or prep table and paint it a contrasting color to create an island.

Add wood or Plexiglas chopping blocks across the section you want to use for food prep and dramatically increase your counter space.

Take a look at the trim pieces that Lowe's and Home Depot feature.

Cabinets should be arranged so that glasses, coffee cups and the items most used are around the sink area.

Plates, serving bowls and other place setting dishes and the larger bowls used for food preparation should be near the stove.

The base cabinets should be used for canned goods, each placed near the area where you keep the proper bowls to prepare or serve the items.

Small appliances and pans should be stored in the base cabinets near the area where they will be used.

The ideal kitchen sports a triangle layout with the sink at mid point, the range and refrigerator across from the sink to complete the triangle layout. This is a step saving and time saving layout.

Your 'Plain Jane' cabinets become rich, new and can even appear Tuscan by adding the corner trim pieces to the base of your cabinet corners and the edges of your upper cabinetry.

They appear to be deep and thick but actually adhere to and wrap the corners of the cabinets; this completely alters the appearance of the cabinets making them appear far more substantial.

Purchase the trim pieces that extend to the floor for Tuscan, Spanish and Mediterranean designs.

The wood is intricately carved or super simple; choose the one that works with your design plan.

Matching decorative trim pieces can be used to replace the tiny one inch trim at the tops of the cabinets.

I picked up two bookcases that were out for disposal because I could not pass them up. They were inexpensive but in good condition.

Shortly after that I had a kitchen challenge that required more cabinet space for storage. I stacked the two bookcases up, and attached at the back with two straight braces found offered by Lowe's for under $4.00 for the set. They were painted to match the kitchen décor.

While visiting a thrift store I happened onto the exact doors I had been searching for to complete the décor. Two vinyl shutters! They were painted in a contrasting color and attached to the wall. For less than $10.00 the problem was solved in an attractive way.

Trims To Change Your Style

     a) Take a long, close look at the toe kickboards (the trim at the bottom of the cabinets by the floor). If yours are wood, paint or touch up the stain if they are scuffed.

b) If your kitchen cabinets are finished with the rubber trim that has been used for many years in less expensive cabinetry, tear it off and replace it.

c) Home improvement stores all offer this very affordably. Pick up a can of adhesive while you're there. You need it in your 'tool kit!'

d) You must have your own tool kit!

e) If you have more than ample base cabinet space think about leaving the doors and hardware off of one set of strategically placed base cabinets; fill the screw holes with wood filler, sand and paint or stain to match the cabinets and add decorative baskets that hold vegetables and fruit.

f) This also works if you have located that perfect accessory table to use as an island (one with a shelf). Look for baskets or containers that compliment your style.

g) This is a space and time saver, providing easy access for food preparation.

h) If you have open wall space that does not offer anything you are interested in using consider this option to add storage and interest to that area.

Check your favorite thrift stores and Craig's List for a hutch that compliments or contrasts with your kitchen design.

Another storage solution:

Anchor the hutch to the wall with screws and add trim boards that match your kitchen trim. Presto! You have a gorgeous new addition to your kitchen. The one pictured here was offered for $50.00 on Craig's List!

Adding an eating area:

If you have a 'breakfast nook' or eat in kitchen consider using a contrasting or matching base cabinetry as your table base by simply adding a piece of glass to the top.

This also works with pieces of furniture such as accent tables if they are the correct height. If you can imagine it, you can make it happen!

Find seating that compliments your design and works for your family at thrift stores.

Adding an office area to your kitchen:

If you have extra wall space in your kitchen, usually near a corner, and need a computer workspace or small office; look for base cabinet drawers or upper cabinets that add a look you want in your kitchen.

Measure the height! Too low is a back breaker and too high will make your arms so tired you never want to come back.

Place one cabinet at each end of the space and anchor them to the wall.

Call local cabinet installers and granite shops and ask about remnant pieces and go out to check them out. They can cut it down for you to fit your space; granite remnants are available in the $100.00 price range.

Use adhesive to anchor the top to the bases.

If granite is not your style, look for glass pieces or narrow table tops that can be disconnected from the legs and anchor the top to the cabinets.

If your desktop is long enough, look for matching or contrasting upper cabinets and anchor them at each end to complete your private office with loads of storage.

If not, look for the compartmentalized shelving units typically used for display and anchor them to the wall above to maximize the use of space and increase storage!

Countertops:

Countertops are at the top of the list of things people hate about their kitchens. They are either worn, burned, dated or just plain ugly.

Consider the following solutions; if these do not seem feasible you may at least have expanded your idea of what changes can be completed easily. If so, apply a fix that feels right to you.

a) Solid surface and granite countertops are the most desirable. If you have them, we will be covering how to treat them in later chapters.

If you want them, then spend some time pricing and budgeting for the installation.

As a rule of thumb; light cabinetry goes will with darker surface countertops; dark cabinetry is compliment by lighter surface countertops.

The exception to this rule is when you want to create a white on white kitchen.

White granite is rare and expensive but there are solid surface solutions that work nicely.

If you are planning a complete remodel of your kitchen all of the tips and pitfalls, including pricing and arrangement, will be featured in the remodeling version of 'Make It Mine', available in the near future.

b) Formica is glued onto plywood to create your countertops. The Formica can be removed and replaced with a new color and design that compliments your style.

Just measure and head back to your favorite online search engine and look for the best pricing. The adhesive is sold at hardware and home improvement stores, typically the same stores that offer the Formica.

c) Stainless steel is sold in rolls. If this is your choice, use adhesive to attach it to the wood that is exposed from removing the Formica.

If you choose not to remove the Formica, you must sand the existing Formica countertop before applying adhesive. If you fail to do this it will pop up in the heated kitchen and become a dismal failure.

d) Strip off the old Formica and install a tile that makes your statement. If you use tile don't leave off the sealer coat when you are finished.

If you fail to follow this advice you will soon notice grout that lifts and falls out or changes color, giving your new countertop a completely different look.

e) Tiling a countertop is not a new idea; however, you can also use 20" pieces of marble and install exactly as the tile is installed.

Pick a complimentary grout color, seal and you have marble countertops.

f) Contemporary and a few other design styles work well with concrete countertops.

While this is more typical for lofts and very contemporary spaces, concrete comes in colors now and a whole new set of design ideas spring from that change. This also requires a sealant.

g) Whimsical designs and cottages work nicely with mosaic tiles on the countertops. Again, peel the Formica off and then buy scraps of colored tiles that match your décor.

Break the tile pieces with a hammer (cover tile with plastic and wear goggles when you break the tiles). Lightly sand the rough edges. These pieces can be randomly placed and glued onto the

Formica, if it is sanded first to create a rough surface for the glue to adhere to.

Finish with a complimentary grout color. This process is less expensive due to the opportunity to purchase remnants of tiles rather than a large group of matching tiles.

Mismatched appliances draw attention to, and age the entire look of the kitchen. Appliance spray paint is inexpensive and the easiest way to match the appliances.

If you are feeling particularly creative you can purchase sheets of stainless coating with peel off backs. Remove handles and anything that protrudes and use a box cutter to cut the sheets to the proper size. Finally, peel off the back and apply carefully, avoiding pressing unwanted seams onto your 'new' appliance.

Or, budget permitting head back to your favorite new shopping spots to steal good deals and to pick up appliances that are well loved and slightly used. My best bargains come from Craig's List; which is probably obvious by this point!

Many builders remove these packages from model homes and offer them on Craig's List.

If your refrigerator currently looks like a scrap book think about moving the catch all magnets and pictures to the side; or purchase an inexpensive small bulletin board and frame those 'special' pieces to really showcase them

Faux Stainless covered Range and Refrigerator

Fixtures:

Lowes and Home depot offer repair kits for porcelain sinks that can make yours appear new.

They also offer plastic sinks that are very pretty and appear porcelain and are heavy duty. I found this shocking the first time I discovered these! The prices, styles and overall look will amaze you. It's not nearly as big an issue as it appears to be.

Last but not least, head to Habitat for Humanity Thrift Store, yard sales, the trusty Craig's List and call local plumbers to see if they have what you need in their back room.

They store the sinks that customers refuse in their back room. You can get a great price from them.

Faucets speak volumes about kitchens. Try all of the above to locate one that does not break your budget and compliments your kitchen. It is the finishing touch. I much prefer repairing or picking up a vintage faucet in lieu of a $20.00 wanna be faucet found in every discount department store.

From blight to a beautiful sight:

If you have a kitchen from the late 70's and 80's that features a ceiling that is intended to mimic a 'cove' ceiling graced by florescent lights hidden behind Plexiglas pieces like the one depicted below, you should be more than ready for a change.

These kitchens do not have a soffit (the drywall above the cabinets) as this is replaced by the lighting design.

If your budget does not accommodate a complete change or you do not have help to tear it out; or, even if your are renting, give some thought to taking down the Plexiglas and covering it with decorative film that matches or compliments your theme.

A rental will require prior permission or your willingness to replace the dreaded Plexiglas with new when you leave.

I am willing to bet the owner will much prefer your look to their previous look so fear not!

You can also use spray paint designed to cover plastic and get rid of those ugly tracks that define and hold the sections of Plexiglas.

This is a beautiful fix to affordably update a really dated idea. Make sure to purchase the transparent version of the film; it is offered in several varieties.

Otherwise you will be looking for your light through a dark cover. This is amazingly affordable!

The film covers pictured here are just a sample of what is available. You can use your search engine to look at the many styles offered.

Online shopping will bring them straight to your door. If you prefer an up close and personal approach head to the nearest Lowes or local home improvement store.

Faux Tray Ceilings created with Plexiglas and Florescent Lighting.

Film Coverings for Cove Lighting

Backsplashes:

Every kitchen needs a backsplash! They protect the walls from grease damage and provide the perfect opportunity to give your kitchen a final treatment that projects your style and design.

Tile is the most common backsplash. It is durable, comes in many sizes, shapes and designs and lasts a lifetime if maintained properly.

If you have granite countertops you will typically have marble tiles to match.

Marble Tiled backsplash

This kind of backsplash is beautiful with any kind of countertop; however, it is an expensive solution.

The simplest tiled backsplash for a novice to install is the 1 inch squares that come with on a 12 x 12 inch mat. Still, you must be prepared to cut tile.

1" Glass block tile

A side grinder is a handheld tool that is capable of performing most tile cuts simply. If you're thinking of the cumbersome wet saws for this job I encourage you to try this first. It is one of those miraculous tips you never want to forget!

Let's examine a few others; Take a good look at the following pictures, notice the 'look and feel' that each backsplash inspires in you.

This is a good test to see how it will make anyone who enters the room feel. Some feel commercial and busy, some cozy and some simply beautiful! Find the one that suits your personal taste.

Subway and larger ceramic tile

Hammered tin

Hammered tin is a quick, decorative and inexpensive fix that can be anchored to the wall and removed when leaving if you are renting your home.

Now you are ready to tackle the windows, flooring and change out overhead and under cabinet lighting with all the tricks of trade we've covered in the previous chapters.

If you are a tenant and the cabinetry is worn you may be able to negotiate a part of your rent to upgrade and make the above changes.

If you are in an apartment community you will probably find that impossible.

But, there is always a way, since 'no does not mean no' you can take down the lighting and fans, remove the hardware and faucets and pack them away in a box and replace with your own. Then add the 'island', space permitting.

I have never, ever moved into a rental property without painting and changing out these items. And, I have never regretted it!

When it is time to move, reverse the process; and head to Craig's List and post a free ad to become a seller instead of a purchaser for any items you no longer need.

Chapter 14
About that Bath!

Baths are next in line for design repair; this is due mostly to the volume of use, wear and tear they must endure.

Baths appear tired because they are tired.

Declining value in a home begins in the kitchen and baths; rendering them the biggest culprit in making homes appear old and in a bad state of repair.

Worse still, the design of the bathroom will place you squarely into the vintage time and place it was built. Why?

Even bath designs have changed dramatically over time. Every 10 years or so, a dramatic new design is introduced.

Walk into a bathroom in a home built before 1950 and you will find a small room with a low bathtub that doubles as a shower, a pedestal sink, tile that ranges from very small 1" tiles to black and white checks on the floor and walls, a commode in front of a window and a wall space to add a free standing cabinet for the bath linens. A second one half bath is usually found 'off the kitchen.'

Walk into a new home built in 2011 and be prepared to be impressed!

The 'master bath' is now the same size as former bedrooms; showers are separate from the roman soaking tub and frequently sport triple or quadruple shower heads and a seat to use while enjoying your shower.

Commodes are much taller and fit for a king (the proverbial throne). They have heated seats, auto flush mechanisms and even a storage in the tank for cleaning chemicals that are, of course, auto dispensed.

Better still, a bidet is perched alongside and both are front and center in their own private room, with a door.

Tile in baths in 2011 range from none except for shower and tub (wet) areas to showers that have travertine marble walls and ceilings!

Long cabinets, much taller (42") than their counterparts from years gone by, line the walls to create a 'his and her space.'

Windows are almost never found near a tub in 2011. Many times windows are located high on the walls to allow natural light to penetrate the room while maintaining privacy.

Skylights still dominate large baths for natural lighting and maximum privacy.

Today's baths have large closets built-in, to house a multitude of linens and provide storage for a 'spa' look and feel in your private space.

It is about intimate time for revitalization.

Your bath need not look like a 2011 bath. It also need not look like a 1950 bath. Our goal is to allow your style and budget to merge with the materials at hand; showcasing them as the very best they can be!

Let's aim for creating a bath that features the things most important to you. Start with the simple and easy things you can change.

a) If your walls are covered in tile half way up on most or every wall, remove it or paint it a color that works for your design.

Epoxy paint will cover the glass tile, remain adhered to the tile and completely alter the look of your bath.

Removing the tile in all areas except the shower/bath area will update your space dramatically and alter the time capsule you are stuck in. This will require scraping the adhesive that anchored the tile, sanding and probably some slight drywall repair that anyone can complete.

In later chapters we will review time and money saving tips and little tricks for completing the simpler, big jobs.

b) Pedestal sinks are a perfect fit for half baths, not so much for master or large guest baths. They offer zero storage, no counter tops and basically just sit there and allow water to pour through.

These sinks are perfect in a half bath; they save space in addition to appearing very sturdy and substantial. Most people associate pedestal sinks with an earlier period in design styles.

c) If your tub is less than your ideal and a replacement is out of the question; look closely at the condition of the tub.

Older tubs are nearly always porcelain, which is fairly easy to patch. The kits are sold at most home improvement stores.

If you have a tub that is constructed from one of the new plastics; you probably never dreamed that it was! Repair kits for these mainly consist of a polymer patch and paint.

The most common complaint about tubs, disregarding the low height, is the buildup of lime and other minerals that have turned the tub either a rusty orange or the grayish lime deposit color.

Even if these appear to be unconquerable; you can wage war against mineral deposits with CLR and Lime Away among other products.

Both of these products are very strong, and have serious warnings for proper usage as do all chemicals. Heed them.

Sometimes harsh chemicals are necessary; they still present a very serious risk when used without the precautionary instructions.

If chemicals are impossible for you to use, take a good look at the citrus or steam cleaning products. The progress may be slower but the benefit is found in the lack of dangerous chemicals. You may have to scrape or use an abrasive pad but, remember tile is glass and porcelain will scratch. Tread carefully with any kind of scraping as a misstep will damage the tile.

In most instances you will be able to remove all of the mineral deposits and shine the tub, faucet, drain and tiles.

I always try this first, and then decide what next step to take regarding the tub and shower area.

If you are interested in trying very long fabric, drapes or sheets for your shower curtain (2 simple and inexpensive spring tension rods lets you easily determine the height for both the cloth curtain and a very inexpensive liner) you will pretty much be able to disregard the tile's effect on your design once it is cleaned.

    Stainless steel inserts are now available. These are screwed into the drywall or a strong adhesive is used to apply to the wall surface.

    Take a look at the new 'looks like tile' insets! Gone are the cheap plastic walls that bent in when you leaned against them! The new inserts come in an array of colors and designs and anyone would be proud to show them off in their new design plan. They are much less expensive then purchasing tile and having it installed and easier to maintain

'A Looks like tile' prefabricated shower insert.

Combine this with the floor tile (pictured) that looks like wood and imagine what you can create!

A little imagination and the willingness to roll up your sleeves or ask friends to help and you will have a 'new bath' pretty easily!

'Looks like wood tile floors'

If you have built in vanities in your current bath and the space is sufficient for your plan, review the cabinetry section of our kitchen makeovers.

Many solutions are covered in that section including painting the original cabinets

It pays off in a big way to jump in and add your own ideas. This method produces the same results in a bath area.

The kitchen cabinetry section offers many other ideas to consider; the effect is the same in the kitchen or bath for cabinetry.

Don't be afraid to try some of these methods. The biggest complaint about painted cabinetry is the RUNS!

If your paint runs, use a very fine grain piece of sand paper and take out the run, wipe off the sanding grit and repaint. Pick up a couple of cans of spray poly in the paint department. This will add a hard, shiny finish that can withstand water splashes and washing.

If you do not have the cabinetry you need, head back to the thrift shopping spots, Habitat for Humanity thrift store and Craig's List where nearly new cabinets can be found at ridiculously inexpensive prices.

The down side of this is the install. If you can handle either hiring someone or doing it yourself, go for it!

If you have a flat mirror anchored over your sink with little screws in plastic caps... tear down that mirror! Normally four screws will anchor the mirror.

Plan on a minor wall repair with your can of patch; let it dry and lightly sand and paint with your wall color.

Decorative mirrors can be found everywhere for every budget. If you have a double sink, hang one above each sink and add wall sconces to properly light the area and complete your design.

If removing the mirror is not possible due to budget concerns or you're living in a rental, think about a Plan B:

Measure the existing mirrors entire surface and hunt down a picture frame in that size or look for thin wood in the desired width and frame your mirror.

Trim is available in every style at your local Lowes or Home Depot stores. The edges will require being mitered which is a little tricky.

Many times I have managed to get the workers at Lowes to make the cuts for me. You MUST be sure of your sizes because if they are wrong, you cannot return the pieces for a refund.

In addition to the countertop tips in the kitchen section, I have many times managed to secure a piece of remnant granite for bathrooms for $100.00. The supplier will also cut the opening if you ask.

This is a perfect time to search for a vessel sink. These sit on top of the countertop with only a small opening for the plumbing.

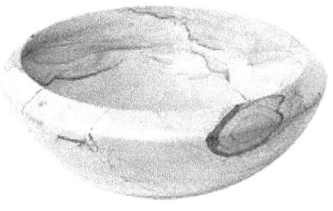

Vessel Sinks

A $100.00 piece of granite with vessel sink

You can also look around your home or in our thrift suggestions and find a gorgeous desk or buffet and have the opening cut out for the sink and plumbing.

If you currently have a very low and outdated commode in your bathroom, go back to the Habitat for Humanity Thrift Store or Craig's list for newly used commodes very, very inexpensively.

If you have decided to keep your current countertop and sink then continue the cleaning process and add your favorite candles or accessories that will instill a feeling of relaxation and rejuvenation.

Commodes are not that expensive when purchased new. If your budget will accommodate one, head back to your favorite home improvement store.

Commodes are amazingly easy to install. They require only a wax ring to seal it and two screws with caps.

Visit the flooring section of 'Make It Mine' for floor solutions. Pay particular attention to the new tile that looks like wood pictured in this chapter.

If possible avoid metal stands that hold towels and other whatnots and opt for large baskets to hold towels.

Another outdated bath accessory is the little wicker or rattan hanging shelving. You'll have a much richer look if you hang a cabinet or wood shelving unit. Glass shelving is also easy to install and works very nicely with modern, classic and contemporary designs.

Opt for an overhead chandelier if possible to complete your knock out bath!

Chapter 15
The First Step in the Journey

Your entry area is a vital space in your home. It is the warm greeting that says 'welcome home' to you each day, the place where new friends gain the ever important first impression and also; the place where people who are not welcome are detained or sent packing! If this is your space change selection, these tips may help you.

Many apartments and some homes do not offer a designated entry area. This is especially true for the 'open space' concept homes.

If you do not have an entry area, take a look at these suggestions:

a) Try placing tall silk bamboo trees on the open side. These trees provide a natural breaking point to designate the size of the entry and yet, still leave slight openings to continue the open concept. Space will determine how many you will line up.

b) Open tall shelving units provide the same visual breaking point as above and allow you to display your accessories very nicely.

c) An entry table or buffet will determine the space in your entry. Place a lamp or other accessory that is tall to continue breaking the space. This doubles as a place to add lighting in your smaller entry areas.

d) If you entry does not have natural light place a mirror on the wall facing a naturally lighted wall. This will reflect the light back to your entry.

e) If you entry is long it is probably darker at the end of it. Try placing wall lighting that travels down the hall and welcomes your guests.

f) Get rid of clutter Shoe racks and tables and chairs are a perfect dropping point for anything that is in your hands. A chair is a good idea, space permitting, as it allows you to seat the people who are not friends and keep them out of your private space.

g) If you live in an area where umbrellas are a necessity, look for a beautiful tall vase to grace your entry and hold the umbrellas.

Visit the lighting section of this book to review lighting details for the entry. Entertain the idea of adding a dimmer switch to your entry light. You can control the look and feel of any space by adjusting or changing the lighting.

Entry halls are one of the few areas that can still sport soft natural wallpaper designs if desired.

If you elect to wallpaper any wall, prepare it properly so you will be able to remove it if you change design styles in the future. Improperly installed wallpaper can wreak havoc in the removal process and damage walls in a way that may require a professional to repair it.

If you are adding an entry table, keep it simple and narrow to allow traffic to pass through unimpeded.

Avoid those cutsy matching mirror and wall sconces that hold candles. Look for things that complement each other and create your own design on the walls.

Vintage candle sticks or candle wall sconces are available at thrift stores. Add these to grace your mirror or pictures to provide a look that far more attractive.

In every instance, if you decide to add a display to your entry table, display items in odd numbered (3, 5 or 7) groupings. The results will be so much more pleasing to the eye than even numbers (2, 4 or 6). It just is!

Clean the door; paint it if necessary or touchup the stain on the door, both inside and out. Your door is the mirror to your home. Show it off with pride.

Chapter 16
Living with Your Choices

The one room most people tackle first in their plan to change design styles is the living room. Now that your guests have cleared security at your entry area, lead the way to the 'Living Room'!

I suppose the name was assigned to this room because of the amount of time we plan to spend in it!

What a tall order; to create a room, a single room, where an entire family can live in it.

Let's do it!

First, measure your wall space and make note of window placement. Write it down; sketch a layout of the room, including doors and windows and their proximity to one another!

Before you decide what furniture will be included in this particular masterpiece of a room, think about it!

Make a note about how it will be used in your family, what things are vital and non negotiable and what things can go if there is a pinch for space or design.

Next, decide on a color to set the tone and mood you want to achieve in this space. A quick trip back to Chapter 4 'Color Your World' will help you select the perfect color.

Remember there are shades and hues of every color; find the one that best suits you and your family, and your plan. You need only to determine what you want this room to feel like before selecting your color.

Next, decide what the focal point of your room will be. This is typically a fireplace, a great view or some area of the room that will hold the most used items like the TV.

In the living room pictured below, the room had 18 foot ceilings; it was a condo with nothing to define it sitting next door to 119 just like it. We added the fireplace from Lowes for $289.00 and hung a free standing cabinet for display above the fireplace.

The opposite wall was perfect for a very large TV armoire and enclosed bookshelves. This provided two focal points, determined by which way you were facing in the room.

We changed out the fans and chandeliers for replacement fans to suit the owner's décor and added lighting on tables and on the floor.

Seaside Cottage Living Room

The owner selected a seaside cottage look for her home. The carpet flooring was replaced with wood, which was sanded and a white bone finish applied.

If you are blessed with a particularly large living room or a combo living room/family room commonly referred to as a great room; you can combine two points of interest in the space.

This is a good example of an owner who took a look at what she had purchased and set about to make it hers.

The point is, never mind what it appears to be when you start, your goal is to make it work for your family and your design style, affordably.

Find your focal point; then begin arranging your furnishings in a manner that will allow the space to be lived in comfortably while traffic moves freely about the room.

Seating should be grouped around your focal point; it should also be arranged to permit conversations between the people in the room.

Avoid overly large pieces of furniture in an effort to make the space fit the furniture. The objective is to make the furniture comfortable in the space.

This allows for the primary focal point and a secondary point of interest that typically includes a quiet time space to read, a desk or some other special area you want to create in the room.

This area should be at the furthest distance from the hub of activity in the room.

Measure the pieces you intend to keep in the room. If you can locate a roll of painter's tape you will be able to measure the pieces of furniture and place them with the tape to see exactly how the floor space and traffic pattern responds to your ideas.

This saves back breaking labor for plans that simply won't work!

If you are using a TV set as your focal point, place it in an attractive setting such as a wall unit, hanging above a media cabinet or on a media cabinet. In other words, make it earn the cherished position of the focal point of your room.

Display it attractively! Add a plant, tree or other accessory beside the area to further designate it as your focal point. Whatever your plan, execute it with pride.

Place your sofa in the area with the largest blank space open that also allows the people in the room to enjoy the focal point.

Leave at least two feet between sofas, chairs and love seats and the coffee table. Anything less is uncomfortable, feels crowded and causes knee injuries and a painful experience in your home.

Avoid the matching sofa, love seat, chair settings. Choose the sofa as your primary piece and then complement it with different colors or patterns that allow all of the pieces to show off. One matching chair or even a matching love seat can be overcome by adding a contrasting piece to the grouping.

Carefully review the flooring, lighting and window covers sections in this book for ideas on how to arrive at the look you are creating.

Examine the idea of adding a sofa table (even if it is a buffet in disguise that will add valuable space for storage, games, etc. that your family uses. When placed at the back of the sofa or love seat it frees up wall space, adds wood tones and a place to add lighting or candles and display space.

I hope you do not entertain the idea of placing your sofa against the wall, in front of the window. So help me that look is the basis of the 'House of Commons.'

It says, "I did not know what to do with anything so I just pushed it against the white walls and lined everything up!" That is not a 'Make It Mine' warriors plan.

Invest in a set of 'moving coasters.' These are available at Dollar Stores, discount department stores and all home improvement stores. The worst job in arranging a room just became a breeze with these coasters.

Pull pieces into your grouping; leave the walls for spectacular wall hangings and accessories.

Don't be afraid to pull the chairs in and angle them to achieve a conversation area. It is uncomfortable and uninviting to have to bend your neck to make conversation with others in the room.

Place the pieces and sit down, have a 'mock' conversation and gently 'live' in the space before selecting the right grouping. You will be a force to be reckoned with if you achieve a comfortable seating arrangement!

People will enjoy their time spent in your home and leave not quite knowing why it was such a good experience. It is called being 'comfortable.'

Personally, I am uncomfortable in spaces where there are no tables; no coffee tables, no end tables, nothing! Just sit right down, hold your coffee and tough it out!

I don't understand this mentality; it inspires people to leave the space quickly.

Carefully examine the rest of your pieces of furniture. Make sure they do not overwhelm the space by excessive height or girth. Every piece beyond the primary sitting area is an accessory. Make them count!

Hang your pictures and wall decorations at eye level. This is somewhere between 5' and 5'6".

Find one place in the room to place your largest wall hanging that will allow it to shine for you.

If you look around your friends' homes you are likely to discover that someone measured about a foot or a foot and a half down the wall from the ceiling and hung everything. It is impossible to balance a room with those kinds of heights. Eye Level, always!

If you want to visually tie a space together, like the seating arrangement, find a rug that is two feet wider than the conversation arrangement and center it on the rug underneath.

If you have a sofa that looks perfect against a wall, look for something that balances the size of the sofa with the room.

As unlikely as it may seem, an oversized piece like the one pictured below will attract attention not only to your prized sofa but also to the entire room as it becomes the focal point.

Eliminate clutter, place only large items on the floor as a part of your décor get rid of fussy pieces that collect dust (a nice curio cabinet is good for these to be displayed).

Your best wall hanging, a flat TV enclosed in cabinetry that can be closed off at will, something that says I'm special!

If you don't see the perfect piece, head to the 'Barely Get Along Street District' in your town! You know what to do!

Add candles in at least one area of your living room. When things are quieter in the house candles are very comforting to relax with.

I think you are ready now to 'strut your stuff' in your living room! Invite your friends and enjoy!

Chapter 17
Into Your Night

Master suites should look and feel special. By virtue of the name 'Master' someone special sleeps there. You!

Typically a master suite centers on the tastes of two people; many times both are very different. The rule of thumb here is to avoid ruffles and severe masculine lines.

The challenge is to strike a balance between a very sensuous private space, the lion's lair, and a restful, harmonious and peaceful place to allow your body to recover and be ready for the next day.

Hopefully you are able to get your partner to join in the paint and lighting selections. Both are vitally important to arrive at the proper conversion of this space from humdrum to spectacular. If they fail to join in, they lose the privilege of complaining!

You gain the home team advantage!

Take a long and critical look at your furniture. Pay attention to the color of the woods and the design. Then start as we did in the living room, with a tape measure and your sketch pad.

Sketch the room including the windows and doorways. Try to arrive at a good perspective of where they are placed in proximity of the entire room. Make notes!

Now, set the practical things aside, close your eyes, and dream. How do you want this special space to feel?

What is important to you? What colors come to mind if you allow yourself to drift past what you have always had to a place you always wanted to go? There now, head to the Chapter 4, 'Color Your World 'section and review what each color inspires.

The Olympic 'South Pacific' and Sherwin Williams 'Smoke Blue' colors make a beautiful backdrop with all white or yellows and teals bedding and linens. Think about the colors and then go online to the paint manufacturer's sites.

You can upload a photo of your actual room (take the picture when full light is available) and then try the colors. This allows you to see your room, with your lighting and your furniture before you jump in to paint. I love these tools!

Look at your overhead lighting. Try to agree on a beautiful chandelier that sets the tone for your new room. Simple or ornate, just select what inspires a fairytale feeling in you and your partner. You do want to escape, don't you?

Overhead lighting makes a huge statement!

Invest $5.00 in a dimmer switch! This allows you to lower the lights, add candles to the tables in the room and drift away together.

Tips to remember:

a) Always place the bed facing the door.

b) Avoid allowing the bed to face the bathroom if possible.

c) Avoid mirrors on dressers or other pieces of furniture that face directly back at the bed. Mirrors capture energy and project it back to the person trying to sleep. You need to escape from unharnessed energy!

d) Add large plants; palms promote a light, airy and romantic feeling.

e) Space permitting, an upholstered bench at the foot of the bed allows for both of you to sit while removing shoes, etc., and also holds blankets and bed linens while you are sleeping.

f) Look for lamps for the nightstands that are a little less practical, more whimsical, for the master suite. Dare to dream and inspire dreams together in the only really private area in your family's home.

g) The master suite should be off limits to the rest of the world! It is your private sanctuary.

h) Heavier wood pieces of furniture, even if they are repurposed, instill a feeling of security in bedrooms. This room is more important than any other to feel safe and protected.

i) Choose window treatments that also can black out the light for those special mornings when you actually get to sleep in.

Look for drapes that can pool onto the floor, making a more romantic statement than tailored panels.

j) No clutter is allowed in this lair! What a bummer to have a beautiful escape littered with shoes, clothes and a multitude of discarded items.

It is so worth keeping your master suite in perfect order! It makes a subliminal statement to your subconscious mind. A 'wow, this place is special' kind of statement.

k) Unless you have absolutely no choice, discard those outdated mirrored closet doors.

Head back to the 'Barely Get Along Street' district if necessary, look for paneled closet doors that continue the message of being in a VIP space.

l) If you have a dresser that has mirrors attached above, think about removing them and hanging them on a separate wall.

Then hang something really special above the dresser that is a reflection of you and your partner. Something you both have an affinity to or a favorite photo blown up into a poster and mounted for special hanging.

m) Try to place the TV in a cabinet or something enclosed; these create more energy interference while you're sleeping!

n) Space permitting, find two chairs that are reflection of the two of you and create a small sitting area to relax with a favorite glass of wine or a great book.

Drape the wall behind the chairs, even if there are no windows. Texture and contrast create a cozy, special feeling.

Have an open discussion about the closet and drawer space. Come to a solution that suites both you and your partner, then keep your agreement.

It is offensive when anyone encroaches on your space, making you feel inconsequential.

Those are terrible feelings to take to your master suite and a really bad place to take a special relationship! Be respectful of the feelings of your partner in this special room.

If you have a master bath, select a color that compliments, not matches your bedroom.

Review Chapter 14 'Splish Splash Time for the Bath' and look for ideas that may work in your master bath. I think every master bedroom and bath should feel like a retreat. This means spa time in the bath.

When this room is completed you will have designed a very special space that is peaceful, harmonious and sensuous! Perfect.

Chapter 18
Guess the Guest

If your new plan is to create sumptuous guest quarters or just a simple guest room, this may help!

Guest spaces are all about comfort. If you're entertaining a friend or family member they either remember the incredible décor, the mattress that allowed them to sleep like a dream or, the week they never slept a wink! Avoid 'Grumble Alley' mistakes in the guest area.

Let's work towards making the best memories from a stay at your home.

The best layout for any bedroom places the bed facing the door. It is the same theory that is in place when entering a restaurant; you always want a seat facing the door. This is an instinctive reaction to the unexpected. It is doubly true when sleeping.

A bed that allows your guest to pile up on pillows and watch TV or read is always a plus. Most guests do not get involved in the family's day to day events and need a get-a-way to allow your family the space to continue everyday activities.

The room pictured below was a typical bedroom enhanced with faux brick on the primary wall. Barn siding was used to create the headboard and then washed with white bone finish to create the lighter effects on the wood.

Chandeliers were hung above both nightstands with a dimmer switch to let the guests set the lighting they are most comfortable with.

Guests don't require nightstands with extra storage, only adequate space to place their traveling clothes and accessories.

The best part of the room pictured is the pillows that invite you to come in and pile them up to get comfortable.

If your budgeting is a concern and you do not have a headboard for your guest space, measure the width of the bed and head to your nearest fabric store.

Look for three or four inch foam which is very inexpensive. Buy enough to cover the width of the bed plus an extra 12" to wrap.

Then check out the remnant table and find a fabric that fits the décor you are working towards in this space. Remnants are very inexpensive and sold by the yard, sometimes by the bolt.

Position the bed and mark off the area on the wall with a pencil. Then use your staple gun and staple the foam to the wall to form a tall and thick headboard.

Once the foam is in place wrap it with the fabric and secure the fabric behind the foam with your staple gun.

You now have an exquisite and inviting headboard that beckons your guests to come and lean into! You can add fabric cover buttons to create the tufted look shown in this picture.

There are online directions to create a headboard by using a piece of plywood, foam, batting to wrap the edges and then fabric to wrap the headboard. There are many variations but the point is; you can create a headboard!

These photos show other people's ideas to create a headboard. Some are foam, hollow doors turned horizontally, oriental screens turned horizontally shutters and even a picket fence! Almost anything can work if you give it a try!

The important thing at this point is locating a good, comfortable mattress. If you are lucky enough to have a furniture liquidator in or near your home they offer very good quality mattresses from hotel liquidations. If not, try Craig's List if a new one is not possible.

Night stands for guest quarters can be purchased at a thrift store. They don't have to match in color or design. Just sand lightly and paint to match your desired décor.

Neutrals like Taupe are the best selections for guest rooms. Regardless of what taste a variety of people have, they all gravitate to warm neutrals.

A small desk that holds a laptop computer and a comfortable small chair is a great addition to a guest space. If you have an extra PC available, hook it up and your guests will brag about the hospitality in your home!

An upholstered chair and table with lighting is another good addition to provide a space to relax without being forced to lie on the bed.

Add wall accessories that create a peaceful feeling; seagulls in ocean scenes, gardens with sunlight, anything that is not busy or harsh will create a restful atmosphere.

All accessories in a guest space can easily be picked up at thrift and consignment stores if necessary.

If your guests have a private bath I am sure they are pleasantly surprised! Opt for a spa like feeling with neutral colors, baskets full of thick towels and candles that invite relaxation.

A small coffee pot and cups with individual packages of cream and sugar are inviting and provide a private wake up treat for your guest.

Overall, this should be a neutral, natural and relaxing space!

Chapter 19
Kids are People Too!

When you are ready to tackle your children's rooms, I urge you to refrain from seeing them as 'just the kids' for a moment.

Try to mentally step into the person they are becoming to help you create a space becoming to, and fit for, a future king or queen!

Children's rooms provide a more restful atmosphere if they are muted shades of your child's favorite colors. If you do not have a separate area for them to play in, avoid bright yellows, reds and oranges if you expect them to actually sleep in there.

Children quickly pick up the subliminal message of energy and those colors promote energy. This makes bedtime a tough sell in high energy atmospheres!

Space providing, aim for a separate bed for each child, a twin is fine or a bunk if necessary. The idea is to provide their own bed for them to claim. It is the beginning of independence.

Your child's room should have a work space for school projects and creative pursuits. Every child needs a room that feels secure, inspires creativity and promotes rest. What a challenge!

Additional storage is a little easier to add in a child's room. You can add small dressers or shelving units to the closet floor enabling them to reach the spaces where they are required to store toys and other personal possessions.

If you fail to address this you will soon discover that their idea of cleaning up their space is to throw everything under the bed where they can no longer see it. Things are relatively simple in a child's world.

Insist on order in your child's room. This promotes learning responsibility which is essential to your child growing into an emotionally healthy adult.

Take them with you to shop for lamps and wall accessories. You will probably have to temper their urges but both of you can arrive at a point of agreement and your child will have participated in his or her own success in arranging their personal space.

These things matter to children who rarely have the final say in decisions at home.

Avoid window treatments that present a 'café' effect. Your child will feel far more secure with thick drapes that close out the darkness and offer a hug at bedtime.

Open the drapes wide in the morning and 'Let the sunshine in!" This is another trick at teaching your child to feel secure in their surroundings.

A small nightlight chases away the scary images a child conjures up in the darkness when they are alone. Let them help you choose one that feels right to them.

Insist on your child maintaining order in dressers and chests and storage spaces in their room. This makes it an easy proposition to let them lay out their favorite choices for school without calling in a search party!

Find a bulletin board that you both agree on for the children's space. This provides a special place to display their work and show it off.

Look for a way to hang mirrors down to your child's level so they are able to see how they look in the choices they have made while dressing for school and other events.

Children routinely fall and get hurt attempting to reach mirrors placed at adult heights. Hanging one on or behind a door is a good way to avoid those falls.

Avoid placing candles or any other accessory in your child's room that promotes fire or any other danger. It is important for them to have their own space; safely.

Chapter 20
It's a Family Affair

If you have a larger home that offers a 'family room' you have already discovered that this is the gathering place for everyone in your family.

These rooms are typically located in the back of the home with easy access to the kitchen and back yard areas.

Your goal is to move the traffic in your home, gracefully, through the space and eventually outside to enjoy fresh air and sunshine.

Most family rooms center on a large TV that allows the family to enjoy special movies or sports together.

Large overstuffed furniture that is comfortable and durable works best in these spaces. Expect family and guest alike to put their feet up, relax and let loose in this space.

Tables in your family room should be equally durable and able to withstand glass rings from drinks and food as many people travel to this room with plate and glass in hand.

Tiled and glass tabletops are perfect for this. Locate some used tables and finish to your desired color and add 2 or 3 coats of poly to seal it or and add your own tiles to create a unique look and feel in this space.

You can also get creative with paint colors in the family room, although, neutrals and earth tones tend to work best here.

Window treatments should be more casual and invite relaxation. Long loose drapes that slide easily open and closed for sliders yet still close out light for special TV programs will be welcome.

Space permitting, a game table is a welcome addition to the family room. This allows people who are not focused on the TV programs to enjoy spreading out with their projects and joining the family while participating in their own activities.

Place furniture in groupings that focus on the activities you expect to be most inviting to your family as they relax and let their hair down.

If you have a combined kitchen and family room space, you can add seating and a place for food that keeps it in the kitchen by adding base cabinets and a tabletop or remnant granite on top to create a bar area. Add seating that you can locate at thrift stores and you have an entirely new look and feel in your space!

Find soft cushions for the sofas that inspire a nap or relaxing with the news or sports.

Larger cushions work best in this space, allowing the younger members of the family to throw them on the floor and cuddle for TV shows.

The family room is all about a comfortable place to do the things you enjoy the most in your spare time.

Plants and trees add to creating a relaxing atmosphere in the room.

Candles should be placed higher so children are not attracted to areas that may be dangerous for them.

Wall accessories should be more casual and can also be more substantial to compliment the larger furniture selections. Then, relax and enjoy!

Chapter 21
Wide Open Places

America has a long history of 'community' connections. It began in our pioneer days when helping one another with protection and ranching was necessary.

Our earliest homes reflect the inevitable 'front porch'. It is an American heritage!

Depending on your location you probably have a porch, enclosed porch, patio or lanai to enjoy the outdoors.

If you want to reconnect with your neighbors or the community, head to your front porch or whatever outdoor space your home offers.

These spaces can and should become an extension of your home. Family members and visitors can spill out onto these areas to relax and enjoy whatever 'nature' your location has to offer.

If you live in a metropolis 'jungle' help is on the way!

A few years ago I went to L.A. on a business venture. My niece lived in Newport Beach, CA so the trip provided some time to 'catch up' and visit with her.

She lived on an upper floor, directly on the beach but facing the street. My impression of Newport Beach is that every street is busy!

At the front of her apartment she had a never used porch that looked out over the traffic and smog.

She was also very unhappy with the layout of her home and was looking for changes that made it more 'user friendly.' Because she was renting she was not interested in spending exorbitant amounts of money to make it feel like home to her.

While she was literally a few short steps to the beach and ocean, she had no way to enjoy the outdoors without leaving her home. She had many friends and enjoyed entertaining at home, not necessarily on the beach.

The challenges for her were the amount of traffic, the lack of any view and for the most part, she found her 'porch' to be utterly distasteful!

We headed to the IKEA store and picked up woven mats in sections of 4' by 6'. These are easy to trim back if you want to cover an entire area since they consist of 1' squares woven together.

Outdoor blinds were available in matching natural colors. We picked up enough to cover her entire open areas without breaking the bank.

Since our choices seemed to be leading towards an Oriental look, we went over to the lighting area and picked up rice paper shades to add to the overhead light and matching shades for the lamps we intended to use out on the porch.

We headed back to her home with our goodies and in a few short hours her never used porch was transformed into a beautiful and usable space.

We hung the blinds and lifted them high enough to allow the natural light in and low enough to afford a private space for her to enjoy.

A quick walk through her apartment led to our gathering pieces of furniture that she would not need after our 'redo.' We added these to her porch décor. We took a little used microwave cart from her kitchen, painted it, inserted inexpensive accordion style fold out wine bottle holders and added it as a wine cart.

Candles and more candles were placed on the tables; two large silk trees were added to complete the cozy atmosphere. Suddenly her unused porch (an urban blight was her description) was transformed into one of the most enjoyable spaces in her home.

Beauty is where you create it!

Early morning hours were spent sipping coffee and reading the paper; evening found her popping wine corks with her friends; sharing cheese and bread over candlelight.

We spent about $200.00 to arrive at this transformation. She became very familiar with her community simply by spending time outside on her porch!

Everything is possible if you allow yourself to explore what you do have, what you can affordably acquire and how it can be used to create the space you desire.

The first order of business is to define the space. Where is it, what activities can it be used for and what would you like it to add to your life.

The small front 'stoop' (this is typically a small concrete pad with a tiny roof over it) may feel very limited to you.

However, you must decide what you want the entrance to your home to say to the outside world and how much it can add to your lifestyle.

The stoop is either going to become a part of your entry; or it will be the entry stopping point for the space you create.

If you elect to simply use it to welcome guests, power wash or paint the stoop and step(s) in a color that works with your exterior color.

If your front door is not the door of your dreams, paint it and shine or replace the hardware.

Add something at the front of your home that makes it distinctly yours. Large pots or yard decorations or plants alongside the stoop extend the eye beyond the small stoop and help you say this is a special place.

Another solution is to head out to your best home improvement spots and pick up paver stones that are very inexpensive. These come in many sizes, shapes and designs; find one that gives a hint as to what is inside the door.

Pick up a couple of packages of black plastic in the paint department of Wal-Mart for under $8.00 while you are out. (Other stores have this plastic but charge twice as much)Add a few bags of sand, mulch or gravel to your list.

Back home you will need to walk off and layout a section of your front yard to create your new space there. Once you feel comfortable about your idea, locate a good rake and remove rocks and large protrusions to create a somewhat level foundation.

Lay the black plastic down across the area you will be using and secure it. (I used long nails several times!) You can trim the paper with a box cutter if you want curves in the design.

You can cut and X into any area where you would like to plant a bush or flowers and dig the hole and plant the addition.

Lay your paver stones out, placing them in a pattern that works for you; then open the bags of sand, mulch or rocks and spread them across the entire area, allowing it to penetrate between the paver stones.

You can add $0.97 outdoor solar lights around the border to create a lighted terrace that leads to the stoop. Add large plants, the seating of your choice and suddenly the front stoop had been transformed into a beautiful entry with outdoor space to enjoy your community. Total costs for this project is under $100.00 if you have available furniture to use outside!

If you have a large porch, clean it and spray or power wash to remove grim that accumulates from wind and weather. You can easily paint it to match your exterior colors if you believe that will help to create your living space.

If not, look at some of the products that can withstand weather, like the inexpensive woven mats. You can separate a small table and chairs from an additional seating area by placing the mats under the table.

Humans are visual creatures. Space looks and feels completely different to us if the eye is broken by a change in color, texture or patterns. It likewise extends what we perceive as the space in any area by the final break point such as a wall or, outdoor, where the design stops.

Use this to your advantage. Create breaks with this technique or extend space by avoiding them.

Porches are a little more secure than an open area.

You can add overhead lighting to create any atmosphere, hang lanterns for effect or even place very attractive, faux wood tables or other weatherproof accessories that are very attractive out on your space.

In every instance, lighting, flooring and placement of the furniture alter the appearance of your space and transform the look and feel you will derive from it. Treat your covered front porch exactly as though it is a part of your home; changing only the things that require weatherproofing.

An enclosed front porch should be treated as though you have acquired a parlor! Refer to the entry suggestions in Chapter 15 in this book.

Lanai's or enclosed patios are typically much larger than porches. Many span the entire length of the home, and are usually located at the rear of or on the side of the home.

If you are one of the lucky people who have sliding glass doors that can be opened to expose the screens behind them; you have the best of both worlds!

Your space can be treated as an indoor space with respect to fabrics and accessories. Glass enclosed porches or lanais can hold wooden tables for games or an outdoor eating experience, an array of overhead lighting to set any mood and can be draped with any material to create a private space when desired.

Tile is usually a good choice on lanais. It can be cleaned easily and works to extend the feeling of an extension of the home.

Enclosed lanai's can be used for real plants or trees since they provide controlled sunshine levels and protection from the elements. They work equally well with silk trees and plants! The following photos show the lanai of a second floor condo on the lake. The room is not large and the owner elected to use paint on the floor, but still managed to create a restful place to share meals and visits with her friends.

On this lanai curtain rods were hung from the ceiling with wire, grapevines were used to bring the outdoors in and fabric shower curtains moved freely to create privacy or allow sunlight in.

Miniature Christmas lights were strung along the top of the wall, creating a romantic and enchanting space to entertain.

Those tiny lights and candle light combined to provide enough light to take the nighttime picture of this lanai.

Ceiling fans are perfect for lanais and covered porches. Choose one that helps to define the look you want to create.

If you have a screened lanai or patio, you can create a living space that offers weatherproof seating without having to choose the typical outdoor lawn furniture with plastic cushions.

The tables shown below were picked up from a restaurant with a Key West theme. We were able to use these to create a beautiful, casual and user friendly space for entertaining.

Children loved the picnic table while the adults preferred the bar tables. You can take any table that fits your ideal, picked up from a thrift store or yard sale and create this look. Find favorite photos, glue them down and apply 2 or 3 coats of poly to weatherproof the finished product.

Add a grill and some wood pieces for conversation areas, trees and plants and your friends will walk away talking about your incredible space!

Outdoor lanterns, low level solar lighting at the center of a group of trees and plants and paver stones can be added to the exterior of base of your patio. This extends the eye to enlarge the area.

Privacy fences can be added but they break the space completely, creating a closed room effect.

Look for large boulders to stack and create an interest point. You can also head to your lumber supplier and pick up two pressure treated 1 x 6 inch boards and several pressure treated 1 x 4 inch boards.

Create a base from the six inch board, nail the one inch pieces into angled slats and then attach the other six inch board to the top. You can spray with Min Wax stain and anchor the wall to the edge of the patio.

You have created privacy, a place for the vines to trail and climb and still have an open feeling in your space.

Most people prefer to paint the patio slab as opposed to tiling it. Your patio is exposed to outdoor wind, rain and snow allowing dirt to pile up and stick to the grout.

Outdoor lanterns mounted to the exterior wall of the home help set the mood in these spaces.

Chapter 22
Crowded Spaces
Lonely Places

When families outgrow their space or even singles make one too many shopping trips, you begin to adopt the idea that 'cleaning' means finding one more place to jam things and close the door quickly before it falls out.

If you have long since tired of trying to cram your 'stuff' into a space that simply won't budge; you may appreciate some ideas to try.

Clutter makes people uncomfortable in your home. It makes you uncomfortable there too. I have tackled this many, many times while helping others claim their space. This is a re-claim in my opinion.

Many times people are offended by the thought that their prized possessions are now grouped into a 'clutter' category. The problem stems from having insufficient special places to let these items show off and say 'I'm special'.

Before we move on to create more storage, take a good, hard look around you. If you cannot see any time in the near future that you will want to display or use the offending items, revisit Chapter 17 and the 'Barely Get Along Street District' in your town.

Your unwanted or unused 'stuff' has value! You will not be nearly so upset at letting it go if you are able to recoup the value. If that is of no interest to you, donate it to a worthy cause in your area. A load will literally and figuratively be lifted off your back.

Back to the task at hand; next, separate things that are seasonal and then separate clothing and items that can be placed in smaller areas.

Your local discount department store sells very large, moving size, zip lock bags. These are perfect for storing clothing and shoes.

Zip the bag shut and it is airtight; your things are protected. Attach the hose of your vacuum cleaner to the bag with a one or two inch opening and flatten it out. These babies are flattened out and are ready to go under the bed!

Unused pictures, posters and anything flat can be stored against the wall behind desks, chests, dressers etc. This keeps them safe and out of sight. (Save that under bed space for bigger items.)

Next, select all the items that you cannot, under any conditions part with; and, you don't want to use in your décor.

These get wrapped with brown packing paper or newspaper and boxed tightly. If you treasure them that much, they are worth packing carefully. Use the smallest possible box to safely accomplish this task.

The top shelf of closets and cabinetry over the refrigerator is a good place for these small boxes.

You rarely use the ends of the top shelf of closet space and almost never open the ones above the refrigerator. Duffle bags help hoist these items to the top in lieu of boxes.

If your closet space in unavailable due to a host of shoes, hanging shoe bags are very inexpensive and free up the floor space in your closet.

Look for low dressers and tables at thrift stores, bring them home, paint and move them into the closet to increased storage for things you need occasionally.

If you have an attic space of any kind, the boxes can also be stored there. If you do not have an attic, larger boxes are a little bit more challenging.

For the larger items and larger boxes, look carefully at the ends of the bottom or floor area of your closet space.

Normally this is a more difficult place to reach into. We tend to hang clothing we rarely use at the ends for this very reason. This space is perfect for larger boxes. Stack them if need be.

You should now be down to the things you either want to show off as an accessory or need accessible to use.

Split them up again, into these categories.

If you have plant shelving in your home (vaulted ceilings almost always offer these) you should consider this area as a built in display area.

It is always high in the air so keep that in mind. Small things will disappear up there. Get creative and ask a friend to help you lift the accessories up to the space.

I have used large pots, birds and bird houses, grape vines, baskets, paintings, dolls and a multitude of other things to make this space special. A contrasting color of paint on the plant shelving area helps to attract attention to the area and the things displayed there.

Large silk plants and items that overwhelm your space can fit nicely there. String the miniature lights across the base of the area and you have an entirely new look.

If you do not have this extra space, look around you. Do you have a corner or an area where you can add it? Shelving wrapped around a room is not the answer; you can however, create a special place, in the air in a corner with glass shelving or any kind of wood that matches your décor.

Corners are rarely used except to stick things in that we don't use. Yours can become a spectacular part of your design, layered if necessary.

If you have an area available in your hallway or other corner to add a piece of furniture that can attractively manage display items, take a stroll through your home and then the thrift stores to locate an inexpensive and good quality piece.

Any piece that has potential can be repurposed to fit your décor! Now your 'stuff' is an essential part of your décor!

Putting things in place, eliminating clutter and freeing up space in your home is well worth the time taken.

Once you complete this process you will begin to notice that friends seem more comfortable, stay longer and enjoy their time with you.

More important, you enjoy your time at home.

If you have a garage, you have an attic most likely.

Your storage problems are more about getting things in order, identifying what will be stored and then determining what method works for your storage space.

In short order, clear the clutter! Bring your house to order! Everything is easier when you eliminate unnecessary challenges in your home.

Chapter 23
Access Accessories

Accessory, by definition, means 'ornament' or 'partner in crime.' Both can apply to your home decor. It's about the display!

When you are searching for accessory items you will be better served by adopting the marine mantra, 'a few good pieces.' This will go much farther to create an inviting and beautiful space than a host of knickknacks and fake silver and gold trinkets.

It has been very refreshing to see trends for home décor move back to appreciating the good quality, barely used treasures from the past.

Large, simple, good quality mirrors grace the walls rather than overtake them. Use mirrors to reflect light and to emphasize a particular piece of furniture.

Avoid placing a shelf underneath the mirror, it adds to the feeling of clutter.

a brilliant reflection

Unless this is a spectacular set from days of old that you really love, don't do it.

Let the mirror make a simple statement, and add accessories to the table. Accessories should be in balance with the weight of the table and the mirror or picture. A fragile, lightweight candle holder will not do justice to heavy antique mirror. Vintage pieces with other vintage items will feel a lot more cohesive.

Accessories are compliments to your room and should not overwhelm the theme.

Choose plants and trees with a completed design in mind. Envision the end result before putting it in place. Use your painters tape to lay out space in your home. Then visually step back and mentally live in the space.

Walk around the room just as you would if the furniture and accessories were there. Get a feel for the flow of the space; then move forward.

Rugs are another accessory that should be well thought out. What are you trying to create? Is the rug slippery when walked across? Is it in a place where children or adults may trip and fall because it is there?

Look at all of these issues and then determine whether it is the right size, shape, fabric and design to enhance your well thought out plans!

Use this same attitude with every accessory! What does it do for the space, for your plan and for the room? Every accessory should have a cause to achieve an effect!

When you are finished, remember that odd numbered groupings (3, 5 or 7) are much more pleasing than even numbered (2, 4 or 6) groupings.

It just is!

Many times we shop and find beautiful pieces, over and over again. Try selecting a few good pieces for the room you are creating and box the rest for a new look later.

More is not always better.

This is true throughout your home. Eliminate dust catching knickknacks or put them into a special cabinet to show them off without cluttering your space.

Regardless of what style you select, all accessories work better with clean, clear and concise lines. Although things may appear to be casually placed, you know for a certainty how much time and thought was put in the careful draping of a piece of fabric!

Children's playrooms and bedrooms are better served by things they can utilize. A hanging chalkboard or bulletin board is useful to them. Pegs on the wall to hold their jackets and rain coats are useful; they are also decorative.

Quick Reference Guidelines

Most new homeowners - when presented with a bare room - are overwhelmed with possibilities and insecurities of furniture arrangement.

They may stand in the middle of the room, shake their heads, and wonder where in the world to start.

Although I can't tell each of you where you should put what furniture, I can give you some questions which will help you think about how you will use your space and some general guidelines for arranging furniture.

How you use your space:

Look at the entrances to the room. Do you have doors? Do they open in or out? If they open in, you will need to allow room for those to open fully.

Do you use the room as a pathway to another room? Is the room a destination room? In other words, is the room one that people go TO or go THROUGH? If they go through, you need an easily navigable pathway from one room to another.

How do you want to feel in the room? Do you want it to be cozy and intimate? Do you want an open and spacious feel? Furniture in a cozy room tends to be places in closer groups. An open feel needs more space between pieces.

Are you going to use the room for entertaining? If so, you need flexibility in your furniture choices. Extra seating may be placed out of the way and be moved into use when company comes.

Furniture Placement Guidelines:

Between the sofa and side chairs, designers normally allow 48 to 100 inches. But you should adjust the space according to your family's needs. If you feel more comfortable with the chairs closer, or if you are better able to hear conversations, then move them closer.

If you are using a coffee table in front of the sofa, the normal placement is 14 to 18 inches from the sofa. But again, if you have short arms or long legs, adjust the table until you are comfortable.

For television watching, the normal guideline is to place the television at three times the size of the screen. But with some of these new big screen TVs, three times the size of the screen is in the next room!

Three feet of space is recommended for traffic lanes. But if you have large family members or lots of kids, I would recommend allow an extra foot for safety for your furniture and for your family members.

In the dining room, an average adult needs a depth of 20 inches for a dining room chair, plus 16 inches to scoot the chair back from the table. Again, adjust the measurements to fit your family.

At the dining table, you should allow 24 inches per person or more. If your family tends to gesture as they eat, as mine does, allow another six inches.

In order to serve your guests, allow 46 inches between the wall and the dining table.

For ideal bed placement, allow at least 24 inches between the bed and the wall to get out of bed comfortably and allow 36 inches between the end of the bed and the bedroom or bathroom door.

As you can see, these guidelines are approximate and should be adjusted for your family. Keep in mind, however, that if you are entertaining guests, your placement will require further adjustments for their comfort and ease of movement.

Small Spaces:

If you can stand in the middle of your room and touch the walls on all four sides, you are going to have to use some magic to add visual space to your room. While that magic probably won't involve the overnight makeover of your space by budget decorating elves, here is some slightly less than elfin visual ideas to help your room look larger:

Light Values: Use light values when painting your room. That does not mean you are doomed to white walls! Try light green or cream beige for a feeling of space.

Vertical Space: Use vertical space for storage. Add a hutch or floor-to-ceiling bookcases as a storage solution to reduce the amount of floor space taken.

Up Against the Walls: Place the larger pieces of furniture against the walls, so the open space in the middle isn't broken up.

Open Arms: Choose a sofa and chairs with open arms and exposed legs. This allows light to filter under the furniture, making the room appear airier.

Scale Down: Consider smaller scale furniture. A sofa or bed that takes up less area will help visually open the room.

Reflections: A large mirror in the room will reflect light around the room. This is especially effective with near a window so the outdoors can be reflected.

Angles: Arrange furniture at an angle if possible. This gives visual interest to the small space.

With some imagination and some rearranging of furniture, you can make any room appear much larger than its actual size.

More Room Design Tips

Furnishing a small dining room can present a challenge, as any small space can be challenging. However, you may very well end up having a more efficient and attractive space since a small dining room can force you to focus on exactly what you need.

Consider Scale

Scale might very well be the single most important factor to consider especially when you are furnishing a small dining room. Your dining furniture should be scaled according to the space you have.

Select a Limited Color Palette

A limited color palette may be a good place to start. It is easier to work with a lighter or neutral color palette as it can make your room look airier.

Contrasting or complementary colors should only be used as accents.

This is the safe approach. If you are confident around colors, a bold color scheme may work just as well. The trick is not to get too fussy, and just keep it simple.

Use Mirrors

A mirror is a small room's best friend. It opens up space like nothing else. Use strategically placed mirrors on the wall. Using more than one can be an even better idea.

Decide on Simple Window Treatments

Simple window treatments help keep fussiness away. Ornate swags and valances could be distracting and too overpowering in a small space. Simple panels could do the job nicely. If you need more privacy, layer with good quality blinds.

Select the Best Table Shape

A round table is the best pick for a small dining room. You might want to pick one with an extension leaf if you have enough space to open it. Otherwise a simple round table will do in a square room.

Pedestal bases are great because you can fit extra guests around the dining table without table legs getting in the way.

A narrow rectangular table might work well in a narrow dining room. The idea is to leave enough space for people to move around easily.

Pick Armless Chairs

Armless chairs work best in a small room as arm chairs require more room. You might also want to pick chairs that have a more slender profile. The idea is to take up as little physical or visual space as possible.

Consider Transparent Furniture

Transparent material such as glass, Plexiglas, or acrylic can make your dining furniture "disappear" leaving you with lots more visual space. Remember, though, that this is more about appearances than anything else. You will still need to measure to make sure that you leave enough space for people to maneuver easily.

Use a Small Profile Chandelier

A large or fussy chandelier could take up too much visual room. Pick something with simpler lines and a small profile. It would make your space appear larger. Remember it is all about scale.

Arranging furniture is mostly about using empty space around your furniture to create flow in your floor plan. You want people to move around comfortably without bumping into furniture and sit down comfortably without grazing their knees or feeling hemmed in.

Living Room

For your living room to be comfortable, make sure you don't crowd your space. Too much furniture crammed into too little space or sparse furnishings in a room that is too large can make for a very unattractive space.

You need to provide enough space for an efficient flow of traffic, and let your space breathe visually.

This creates a sense of well being and relaxation.

Traffic Lane: 3' or more

Foot room between sofa or chair and edge of coffee table: 1'6".

Floor space in front of chair or sofa for feet and legs: 1'6" to 2'6".

Dining Room

To enjoy your dining room to the fullest, make sure you leave enough space around the table so that people can get in and out of their chairs comfortably and the person who is serving can move around the table without trouble.

Space for occupied chairs from edge of table to back of chair:

1'6" to 1'10"

Space to get into chairs: 2'6" to 3'

Traffic path around table and occupied chairs for serving: 1'6" to 2'

If you're using armchairs, remember to add two inches to the measurements.

Bedroom

In a bedroom, place furniture so that you don't stub your toes should you need to get up in the middle of the night.

You should also be able to move around comfortably to make the bed and be able to open any drawers without trouble.

Space for making bed: 1'6"

Space between twin beds: 1'6" to 2'6"

Space in front of chest of drawers: 3'

Getting into or out of bed: 2'6"

Around the House

Leave enough space around the doorways, or the room may look very unwelcoming, and crowded. You always want to leave a small transitioning area uncluttered by any furniture when moving from one area of the home to another.

Space from doorway to first object: 3'

Space around main entrance: 4'

Just because you live in a small space it doesn't mean that you have to use small furniture. You will find that many times, using large pieces when decorating small spaces can actually make a room look larger, rather than smaller.

Using a lot of small pieces of furniture can make it look like you're trying to cram too much in and the room can end up look cluttered and cramped. The key to keep this from happening is to use large furniture, but just use less of it.

For example, in a tiny living room rather than trying to fit in a sofa, chairs, ottoman, coffee table and side tables, try using a sofa, a single table or bench, and perhaps a single side chair. If you have the space you can even include a large armoire for storage.

Get rid of excess small pieces and instead include only what you'll actually use. Then try to open up the space with an oversized mirror on one wall (if you can get it across from a window so much the better).

It sounds crazy but it works. Before trying it out; draw up a floor plan on some graph paper or use an online floor planner to experiment with furniture placement.

Simple fixes for small spaces can help you maximize every single inch of your home. The three things that you most need in a small space are function, comfort and style so before you buy anything make sure to look for pieces that provides these three.

Go Vertical: Consider investing in tall furniture. Floor space is precious, and by going upward instead of outward you give yourself extra room.

Use Walls: By adding shelves or wall mounted cabinets you give yourself room for display or storage without using up extra floor space.

Stylish Storage: Buy occasional and coffee tables that provide storage with drawers and shelves. Beds, room dividers and ottomans are some other pieces of furniture that can provide you with extra storage.

Decorative boxes and storage bins can also store seasonal clothing, sporting goods, office supplies or anything else.

Stackable Chairs: Stackable and folding chairs are an excellent way of keeping a supply of seating that you can pull out as you need.

Retractable Doors: Retractable doors that don't open out let you fit armoires and entertainment centers in small spaces with ease.

Try the Kids' Department: Creative use of youth furniture can serve you well as it is designed to fit into smaller rooms. It can also accommodate most adults just as well. For instance, a child's dresser or desk can fit into small areas. And with today's wide selection of styles you are bound to find a piece that matches your own.

Look for Wheels: Many pieces of furniture have wheels, upholstered ones as well as tables and shelves. The ability to easily move your furniture around to where you need it can serve you well.

Consider Leaves: A full-size dining room table might be too big for your dining area. Look around for one that has removable or retractable leaves.

Even though all of these issues were covered in various places in this book, a handy dandy reference guide makes things move swiftly if you're in a bind!

Chapter 24
Tools of Our Trade

This little pink tool kit is sold in most online bookstores and a host of other options and add on's available. You can also head to Harbor Freight, if your city has one, and find unbelievably good deals on tools.

Or, of course, you can and should shop at the stores and sites that you are familiar with that have great prices!

Regardless, YOU need a tool kit!

A good heavy weight hammer, a battery powered screw gun, a nail gun, tape measure, at least two rolls of painters tape, glue gun, coaster to move furniture, paint brushes and rollers and a small and medium size level are essential to any homemaker!

These tools have nothing to do with plumbing, electrical, HVAC or any other BIG job.

These tools are necessary to properly hang a picture, layout a room, or to determine the size of drapes, pictures or anything else you intend to hang or display.

Yours does not have to be pink or matching anything, it does have to be filled with the proper tools and you need to learn how to use them!

If you have no experience at all, find a friend, male or female who can help you learn. If not, ask the sales clerk when you purchase them.

You are unstoppable with your trusty tools and the tips you have learned in this book!

Carry On!

Chapter 25
Know When to Fold 'Em!

We've spent a lot of time discussing how to make existing things work. Now, for the diehards with a bigger vision and who insist they see a better way; we're with you.

If you see a wall that simply makes no sense to you and are determined to tear it down by yourself, you better know the history on that wall!

Load bearing walls support your roof. Every exterior wall and some interior walls are load bearing.

Not that you cannot ever remove one, but, a support beam that meets your building code must take the place of that wall when it is moved. (At the same moment)

This is not a guessing matter. If you are sure you know but have a tiny doubt you need to make a quick trip to your attic and check things out.

Up there it is very clear which walls are supporting the roof. Learn to love them or call a building contractor. If you fail to do this you will still be calling a contractor. It is much less expensive this way.

More than one homeowner looks at the placement of a wall and wonders what the heck was in the mind of this builder! It is more common than you might imagine.

Walls in your entry that separate your living area are almost never a load bearing wall.

However, in older homes where roofing trusses were not used, the kitchen is in the back of the house and the living area in the front; and you guessed it, a load bearing wall separates the two.

This is the wall most people want to move or eliminate to expand space.

Check with your county building department before making changes. An owner builder permit is inexpensive, allows you to hire sub contractors and gives you the benefit of the dreaded building inspector.

If you are dealing with a contractor or sub contractor who hates the inspector or frequently talks about getting around the code; you need to win this battle with your shoes and walk away.

The building inspector is on the scene to protect the occupants of the home or building. Anyone who wants to avoid the inspector is cutting corners and not meeting the safety code. These people are your FRIENDS, even when you don't like what they say. Regardless, you will meet their guidelines or tear it out.

Quick Stepping!

Recently I went through an open house in a very nice subdivision in south Florida.

The home had a large enclosed pool and had been built with a large lanai surrounding the pool.

Somebody who previously owned the home decided to add some square footage to the house by adding a wall across the lanai. Things were probably going really well as it showed nicely; until you opened the slider doors and found a 12 inch clearance before hitting the water in the pool!

I'm sure the home is going to be on the market for a long time. Even then, an appraiser will come when a new buyer attempts to get a loan and the wall will come tumbling down.

Staying within the guidelines of the building codes is a good idea. One way or another, you're gonna do it!

Every community and state is different; for the most part you are safe making painting and interior changes that do not move walls, electrical, plumbing and most HVAC (heat and air) changes without the benefit of a permit.

You can landscape your lawn so long as you do not add plumbing (sprinklers, fountains or pools) all of which may require a permit.

Check your county building codes (posted online) or call the county building department. They are usually happy to tell you up front rather than be called out to make you remove something.

Guess who knows more about the contractors and sub contractors than anyone in your area? Yep, it's the building inspector. He cannot recommend anyone but the expression on his face is very telling.

Better still, you can go to the board of professional licensing in your state and check the complaints that have been filed against any licensed individual.

You're not helpless or a victim unless you choose to be.

Get bids; at least two unless you are sold on a particular contractor's ideas and have seen their work. If that is the case you should negotiate to a price you both feel is fair.

Be present when the inspector comes. You can learn more than you wanted to know by his visit.

Remember, I have been on both sides of this coin, have remodeled homes, sold homes and built homes; I say this is so you will understand the next statement:

Once you have established a relationship with your contractor or sub contractor that you feel good about; get off their backs!

They are overloaded with ensuring that materials are delivered and people who work for them are on the job. They get paid when it is finished.

Anything you are paying prior to the end of the job is for materials and meeting the payroll on your job. Let them do their job. They desperately want to be paid for their work! I promise.

What to do if things aren't going so smoothly? Stay calm. Schedule a meeting with your contractor and take notes. Write down your questions and the answers you are provided.

Ask them to review your notes to ensure that you have correctly taken the information. Date it, insert the location and time of the meeting, ask them to sign it for you and put it into your file.

You have correctly executed a legal document that can be assumed to be a part of your agreement with the contractor.

If things don't improve and you have reasonably allowed the contractor to perform, call another contractor to look at the job. Unless it is terribly botched, a good contractor will not attack another contractor's work.

He may point out things that could be different. If it is really as bad as you feared, you're going to need a new person on the job anyway.

If you determine this to be the case show the new person the notes taken at your meeting.

I want to again caution you not to jump the gun and assume your contractor is worthless and ignorant because you don't like the pace of the job.

They want to finish more than you want them to finish. If things are not moving along, try to rationally determine the reason for delays.

If something is beyond the control of your contractor due to back orders etc. it is also beyond your control. Just relax!

Early in this book I mentioned the method that my brother, the building contractor used in his business. You may recall that I told you he 'walked through a day in the life' of the home buyers. Think About It!

One day I brought a couple to see him who had a specific request regarding the dining room. They had purchased a table that seats 12 people and were determined to make the house fit that table!

As I said many times, anything is possible. As we sat around the table my brother looked for the best response to their concerns.

At last he said "Let's add a bay area to the dining room." This would add 5 feet of usable space if the table extended to the bay window. The bay area would cost an additional $4500.00. I thought that was a lot of added expense to accommodate a table.

The owner was insistent that she did not want a mere extension; her dining room was important!

At the end of this meeting, after a great deal of discussion, the owner decided to extend the entire front of their two storied home to accommodate the table. The cost was a walloping $30,000.00!

I personally thought this was foolish, it still bothers me today. I hope the table is a sturdy one that they will use for years to come at that price for the accommodation.

Use your head, not your heart when you are dealing with extensions or changes to your home. If you get caught up in the dream phase you will hit the ground with a resounding thump when reality meets you there!

Contractors can make anything happen that you can dream of. Don't tread so far out into the water that you will need a tug boat to get back to dry ground!

Be reasonable, consider costs and the value added and then proceed.

Chapter 26
The Hero in You

Most people know exactly what song was popular when any major event happened in their life.

Music is 'soul food,' it inspires us to let go and to feel. Music has no boundaries; it creates an atmosphere or sets a mood. Music is like an emotional playground. It is also particular to every individual. We all know what makes us feel good and we turn to music under all kinds of conditions.

But, did you know… music opens the channels of creativity in your brain? The purpose of this book is to help each person find their own niche in creating a space that is perfect for them; not perfect for a designer, just perfect in their lives!

Everyone is creative; many people just don't tap into that part of their mind. It is a closed door that music slowly opens! So, keep playing the music while you work!

I have to imagine this is where the 'whistle while you work' idea sprang from.

My mother had 6 children. She also maintained a perfectly clean house. Every Monday morning she faithfully removed the old wax from all the hardwood floors and applied new wax.

There were mountains of laundry involved in a household that size. Dryers were not prevalent back then. My mother carried laundry out at 6:00 AM, even on the dark winter mornings, and cheerfully hung the clothes out to freeze dry.

I love homes. I love almost everything about them. I could not, however, understand why in the world anyone would work as hard as she did and never complain.

She made our clothes, taught Sunday school classes, directed the choir and finally went to work at a large newspaper and quietly and without telling us so, was awarded the Governor's Award for Excellence in Journalism.

One day I finally asked her, "Why don't you EVER complain?" It was not natural! I helped as much as I could, we all did, there was just too much to do and still, she did it.

Her response was so simple, "Instead of being resentful, I work for God and for my family that I love."

She said she had never thought much about the volume of work, only that she was thankful to have a home that she could make her family comfortable in.

Maybe most of us feel that way about our parents or someone influential in our lives. They seem to maintain standards that are always a beacon of light in the dark.

My mother played music all the while she was sewing, cooking, canning and getting the next class ready or disciplining all of us children.

I swear it made her smile, and she was anything if not creative in her methods of making us look for a better way to handle the jobs she insisted we do.

We have all heard the axiom that the longest journey begins with the first step; I believe it is begins before that.

I believe that when something matters to us a lot, we harbor a dream, so dare to dream. The dream fans a tiny flame, a pilot light that ignites hope. Hope springs to life when we begin to believe that there might be a way to accomplish the dream. Once we believe in the dream, we begin to realize that dream.

It is then that the first step in a long journey begins. I appreciate your joining me on realizing your dream. I hope your 'How to Turn Mundane into Magnificent' experience has provided helpful ideas and information for you to live by and with.

Having a home is an American heritage; having a home you love is an American dream! We're a nation of dreamers, movers and shakers! There's a hero in you! Dare to Dream!

'You can't hide your secret thoughts; they keep showing up as your life."~ Michael Beckwith

About the Author

Alexa Keating is a healing/transformative author who currently has 32 books available to the readers and 500 articles published. She has earned a well-respected reputation as a commercial and residential Design Specialist with a career that began in 1976 and continues through today.

Her home creations helped to create winning residential development projects from Ohio to Florida, most notably remembered by her ability to work with each home buyer to create a home that reflected their unique personality showcased in an elegant and natural design.

Alexa's commercial designs included award winning and much celebrated retail store window and floor displays that were photographed and filmed by an international audience while frequently drawing gasps of surprise and awe, always bringing unsurpassed sales.

Her notable skill in conceptual decors has earned her a reputation as a premiere decorator. Her work was noted in Who's Who in American Women in Business, Finance and Industry over several years. Alexa's passion for home decor is reflected in the beautiful surroundings that she creates.

Her ability to collaborate with architects, her own group of contractors, and her clients have earned Alexa a well-deserved reputation as a true professional.

Born and raised near Cincinnati Ohio and re-locating to Florida in 1999 she continued her pursuit of decor and real estate development in Fort Myers and throughout south Florida, now

'Sign It' is an in depth guide to redecorating your home according to the birth sign of the occupants by using harmony and balancing energy to inspire and nourish the occupants to be the best they can be.

Visit Alexa's website at arkconnect.com to preview her books and articles now available

Alexa Keating

www.ingramcontent.com/pod-product-compliance
Lightning Source LLC
Chambersburg PA
CBHW070626290526
45790CB00001B/8